The Game Plan

The Connection Between Sports and Financial Success

BRYTON W. KEYES

Ryan & Mandy
I hope you enjoy the read!
"swing for the fences"

Copyright © 2020 Bryton Keyes

All rights reserved.

ISBN: 9798674484721

DEDICATION

To Erik. Invest wisely.

To my love, Kristyn. It's your belief in me that makes dreams possible.

TABLE OF CONTENTS: PLAYBOOK

1	Introduction – Personal Finance and Sports	1
2	Cash Flow- Listen to Coach Popovich	7
3	Saving – Unless Your Dad is Mike Trout	13
4	Debt Management – The Kentucky Way	23
5	Surviving College Years – Rookie of the Year	33
6	Super Bowl Investing	45
7	Compounding like Auston Matthews	54
8	Asset Allocation/Diversify- Team World	61
9	Halftime- What to Do if You Haven't Saved	69
10	Risk Management – Control What you can	76
11	Estate Planning – What Happens Next	82
12	General Manager- It's Okay to Ask for Help	92
13	Competition- Stronger and Faster and Luckier	99
14	Patience – Why Leaf Fans would make great Investors	107
15	When the Game Plan Changes	114
16	Know the Rules to Win the Game	119
17	Hanging up the Jersey - Retirement	126
18	Putting it all Together	135
19	Last minute of the Game	140
	References	146

ACKNOWLEDGMENTS

To my wife Kristyn, thank you for believing in my dreams, challenging me, expecting the best of me and loving me always.

To my editors, thank you for taking the time to read through countless copies of this book. Your input and guidance has brought this book to life!

To my family, I wouldn't be here today without your support, encouragement, and love and understanding. Thank you.

1. INTRODUCTION
(PERSONAL FINANCE AND SPORTS)

"You miss 100% of the shots you don't take"
-Wayne Gretzky, Michael Jordan, Every Sports Dad Ever.

THE GAME PLAN

Sports have always allowed me to see things in a different light and provided analogies to understand and learn important concepts. Even though you might not participate in a particular sport, you may still use phrases like 'playing hardball', 'let's touch base', or saved by the bell'.

These phrases aren't just reserved for sports talk but are becoming more and more a part of everyday conversation. Have you ever been a part of a conversation where it suddenly feels like you're on the set of ESPN? One minute you thought you were explaining what you did over the weekend and the next, you are chatting with Shaquille O'Neal and Charles Barkley providing the halftime report. Sports can provide a unique approach helping explain concepts to people in many different ways.

What about personal finance? Do sports offer relevant lessons on how people can improve their spending, cover their risks and invest more wisely? I know that sports can bridge the gap between this abstract financial world and reality. That's the goal of this book; I want to take personal finance topics and concepts and put them into a sports situation that not only helps explain the topic in a simpler way but also makes it more fun! Because yes, it's time to make personal finance fun and easy to understand for us everyday normal people.

Too many people pay little to no attention to their finances and where their money goes. This is something that can destroy people over time and prevent them from achieving the goals they want to achieve in life. We work so hard for our money; shouldn't we make it work just as hard as we do? It confuses me how people work so hard for their money but then throw it away without the same care they took to earn it. It's time we start understanding where our money is going and be careful with where it goes. It's time to start making our money work for us.

In an age where it is easier than ever to search the Internet for financial advice, it is tougher and tougher to work through the clutter and the right information. It's time for people to become more knowledgeable about money because currently our society lacks knowledge on the basics of personal finance. It's time for this confusion to make more sense. It's time to get in the game.

A study (Anderson, Baker, & Robinson, 2016) that was published based on responses from more than 5,800 LinkedIn members in 2014, finance professors Anders Anderson of the Stockholm School of Economics and David Robinson of Duke University asked basic questions testing how much people knew about investing and personal finance.

One question asked: "Imagine that the interest rate on your savings account was 1% per year and inflation was 2% per year. After one year, how much would you be able to buy with the money in this account?" (Anderson, Baker, & Robinson, 2016)

(The correct answer: "Less than today.")

Only 38% of those surveyed got all five questions correct. Even worse, more than one-third of chief executives, chief financial officers and chief operating officers didn't get all the answers right.

Worse still: The study asked people to estimate how likely their answers was to being correct.

Those who got no more than two of the answers right estimated, on average, that they had gotten 2.5 correct. Many who got none right thought they had nailed every question.

Confidence is great for succeeding in many areas of life but when you become overconfident or even cocky in your abilities, it can be detrimental. We all remember that cocky athlete that actually had no skill to back their mojo. The one that would talk a big game only to try some hero move and get stuffed and sat on the bench the rest of gym class. It's great to be confident but let's start developing the skills and knowledge to make smarter decisions with money. It's great to be confident but let's start developing skill behind our confidence.

"People who lack financial literacy are just as likely to be sure of themselves as those with high financial literacy, but their confidence is likely to be unfounded," says Prof. Robinson (Anderson, Baker, & Robinson, 2016).

Everyone wants the secret, the key, the roadmap to the golden path that leads to the Holy Grail: the magical low-risk, high-return investment that can double your money in no time. Everyone wants to chase the returns of whatever stock has been hottest and to throw away whatever has gone cold. People want to hold on to the idea that there is a way to become a millionaire overnight.

As you'll find out, an overnight millionaire is a fantasy unless you win the lottery (or you are the number one pick in the NFL/NBA/NHL draft). Accumulating wealth takes time and there are many simple things you can do to increase your wealth.

A book that doesn't tell you how to become an overnight millionaire? What's the point?

The heading above–to be clear, is meant to be sarcastic. No book can make you an overnight millionaire. However, by taking the concepts in this book and applying them to your personal financial situation it could actually make you a millionaire (it just may take a couple years rather than at the stroke of midnight).

Being in control over your finances is more important than ever before, especially due to many factors such as:

- The decline of defined benefit pension plans
- Increasing life expectancy
- Less long-term job security and more contract work causing more uncertainty
- High amount of student debt
- High housing prices
- Low-return environment

In order to meet basic goals like retirement or buying a house, people have to save and invest on their own and make sure they avoid common mistakes that hurt long-term results. To build wealth, young people must start investing early and those who have accumulated wealth need to preserve and use effectively. This book will be your playbook to financial success. Time to get off the bench and get in the game. Let the training (or games) begin!

2. CASH FLOW
(LISTEN TO COACH POPOVICH)

"Don't save what is left after spending but spend what is left after savings."
- Warren Buffett

THE GAME PLAN

Gregg Popovich, head coach of the NBA's San Antonio Spurs is regarded as one of the best and most respected coaches in NBA history. "Coach Pop" earned that reputation by leading the small-market San Antonio Spurs to five NBA championships and being named NBA Coach of the Year three times. He consistently has one of the best teams in the league earning an NBA record 22-straight winning seasons. He is easily one of my favourite NBA coaches not only because of his success but how he achieves his success. He runs his teams based on an unselfish, extra-pass, find-the-open-man, hard-nosed defence that has been dubbed by some as "The Spurs Way." One of my favourite things about "Coach Pop" is his honest in-game interviews.

During a regular season game in 2016 with his San Antonio Spurs trailing the Miami Heat, 24-20, after the first quarter, the Popovich stepped aside quickly for an interview on the side-lines (Duffy, 2017).

When asked about his impressions of the quarter Pop simply stated, "We're behind, and they're ahead."

"How come?"

"They scored more than we did."

They scored more than we did. Huh? Seems like an obvious answer to the question on why the Spurs were behind but makes perfect sense. In sports, the object of the game is to score more points than the opponent to win the game. It is a simple concept in which there can be many different strategies for achieving winning results. At the end of the day, you just need to find a way to score more points than the other team and find what works for you.

The same rings true for building wealth. In fact, the formula for accumulating financial success is no secret. Spend less than you make, and you will increase your wealth. It's a simple concept that comes with powerful results. And unless Patrick Mahomes is going to buy you a house or you win the lottery, the way to start increasing your net worth is to save regularly and invest a portion of your income. Then leave it to the magical power of "compounding" to allow your invested savings to grow exponentially over time (which we will look at later on). Conclusion: the more savings you have invested over a long period of time, the greater your net worth will be.

One way to increase your net worth is to gain better control over your expenses. A great way to do this is with a personal or family budget. Listing the amounts of money, you expect to receive and pay out will allow you to realistically assess your cash flow and help prioritize your spending. Most people don't have a real grasp on what they're spending or what they're bringing in, and quite often people are spending more than they're bringing in without really realizing it, thus creating severe financial problems over time. This is pretty typical given the consumerist lifestyle that so many of us live. However, the exercise of preparing and sticking to a budget will help with deciding where and how to reduce expenditures.

A very practical budget system is the 'cash envelope strategy'. Each week write your budgeted amount for daily expenses on an envelope and put the cash allotted in the envelope. When the cash is gone for that expense you're all out. This is tough in the early stages when the cash runs out and we still have our spending habits but it very quickly becomes natural just like those new leg day workouts. They hurt for the first couple weeks but it all pays off in the end, this time literally.

Many of us think, 'we just need to be making more money in order to increase our net worth. I mean look at those millionaire professional athletes. They can own anything they want: fancy cars, private jets, and massive homes'.

While the super rich can afford to purchase expensive luxuries, the most successful people know that living within their means is the path to sustained wealth. In other words, just because you can afford the more expensive option doesn't mean it's always the best choice. Similarly if you buy the best golf clubs it doesn't mean you become a better golfer, you just have really expensive clubs to hack up the course with. Same goes with your money, don't spend more than you're making.

As the saying goes: A penny saved is a penny earned. If you spend simply because you can, you can end up with an empty piggy bank. There are many examples of "former millionaires" blowing all their money on things that add no value to not only their net worth, but also their day-to-day lives. No-one wants to be known as a "former millionaire" and the only person that doesn't want to be a millionaire - is a billionaire.

The thing is, whether you're making six figures or just scraping by, the principle of spending less than you make is the cornerstone of building wealth. Live on what you need and put the rest to work.

Billionaire investor Warren Buffett is a prime example. The guy is worth $77.7 billion dollars. $77.7 BILLION DOLLARS. Yet Buffett still lives in the same house he purchased for $31,500 ($260,000 in today's dollars) in 1958, uses coupons and never pays more than $3.17 for breakfast (Elkins, May 2017).

Buffett's not alone, either. Even though NFL running back Alfred Morris earns millions, he still drives a 26-year-old Mazda 626 Sedan from 1991 that he bought for $2 (Mazda, 2017). Washington Redskins quarterback Kirk Cousins earned $20 million last year, but he chooses to live in his parents' basement with his wife during the summer and drive a dented GMC Savana Passenger van that he bought from his grandma for $5,000 (Elkins, September 2017).

One of my favourite stories is Daniel Norris, an MLB pitcher for the Detroit Tigers who is one of baseball's best young talents. He has a consistent 92-mile-an-hour fastball, seven-figure bank account, a $2 million signing bonus, a deal with Nike and a growing fan club, yet he spends his off seasons living in the back of a 1978 Westfalia camper he purchased for $10,000 (Saslow, 2015). Despite having a large amount of money to allow him to live a crazy, extravagant lifestyle, He decided to spend his first offseason vacationing not on a Caribbean cruise with teammates or partying in South Beach but instead in the hostels of Nicaragua, renting a motorcycle for $2 a day, hiking around the jungles and surfing the ocean waves (Saslow, 2015).

ESPN Magazine gave an example of Norris' frugality when he was with the Blue Jays in 2011. It said that his $2 million signing bonus finally cleared when he was in Florida with the rest of the Blue Jays' new signees. All of their bonuses had been deposited on the same day, and one of the players suggested they drive to a Tampa mall to splurge. They shopped for three hours, and by the time the spree finally finished; most of them could barely fit their haul back into the car. Most players had spent $10,000 or more on laptops, jewellery and headphones. Norris returned with only a T-shirt from Converse, bought on sale for $14. It's been a fixture of his wardrobe ever since (Saslow, 2015).

Norris, Buffett and many other successful people have something in common. They realize that buying the most expensive car or shiniest jewellery actually won't make them live any longer, bring eternal happiness or be any better of a person. Using their resources to create value and use for meaningful experiences is actually the key to building wealth. It can be difficult to resist the urge to spend, but once you make it a habit, it sticks. Then when you do splurge on a nice meal or flowers for your wife, it's because you have been saving and it feels even better.

In the end, building wealth comes down to these radical ideas:

Spend less than you make. Save. Invest your savings. Live simply. Use only what you need. With those thoughts in mind you will never have trouble with cash flow again?

3. SAVING
(UNLESS YOUR DAD IS MIKE TROUT)

"Champions are champions not because they do anything extraordinary but because they do the ordinary things better than anyone else."
- Chuck Noll

Saving is hard. There are so many things to buy. So many reasons you feel like you just don't have enough this month to set aside. I mean, it's not your fault the human brain wasn't built to be the perfect money-saving machine. But unless you're the heir to Roger Federer's estate, your best friends with Naomi Osaka or Mike Trout is your dad, or you never want to retire or buy a house; you're going to have to figure out how to do it anyway. If you think you can wait until you're older, than you do not understand the concept of compounding or that saving a little bit now is smarter than saving a lot later (more on that in Chapter 5).

When you think of choosing between making a little quick money now or growing rich later, we all know what the right answer is supposed to be….be patient and hold out for the bigger gain. But when faced with a real-life choice rather than imaginary, that fast money can seem irresistible. New research is helping to explain why your brain is much more aroused by $1 today than by $1 tomorrow. And $1 six months from now doesn't create much incentive (Zweig, 2016). These studies have helped provide reasoning to why we make such impulsive decisions that are inconsistent with our long-term goals.

"When our emotions are charged, we have a hard time waiting for a reward," says Carnegie Mellon University's George Loewenstein, who conducted a study on people's choices and their brain activity (McClure et al, 2007). Even the chance of getting a slightly bigger reward tomorrow doesn't have the same stimulating effect on your brain as a gain today does.

Same situation plays out in the sporting world. There have been countless occasions where a general manager has come into a team promising a quick fix and a championship team only to grab some high-priced players who fizzle out and then tread water again (ahem Brian Burke and the Toronto Maple Leafs…).

So, if our brain is wired like this, are we forever doomed as savers or are there ways we can improve? Maybe a couple sports analogies can help show the power of sticking to a plan.

Let's start by using the NHL's Chicago Blackhawks rise from the bottom of the league to their modern-day dynasty in the years 2007-2015.

The Blackhawks had once been the most popular sports team in Chicago, but in 2004 it had been named by ESPN as the worst franchise in sports. They were a mess in many areas, from their front office to the team on the ice so they knew if they were going to be successful they would have to create a plan and stick to the process. It was going to start slow but in the end it paid off. Same situation plays out when you are saving money. You start with a little and continually add on top of the base and over time, you gain wealth.

Building a Base - Through the Draft and Paying Yourself First

Chicago started their road to success by building through the draft. They carefully selected the players and management that slowly turned into a powerhouse line-up.

Every championship team needs key players for different positions. The Blackhawks first shored up their defence when they drafted Norris Trophy winner Duncan Keith who could play solid offense and defence every night.

The next year they drafted players such as defenseman Brent Seabrook and goalie Corey Crawford who turned out to be Olympians and all-stars respectively.

Chicago's transformation began to gain steam when in 2006 they drafted future captain Jonathan Toews. Arguably the best two-way player in the game, he is a defensive player of the year and elite scorer.

The following year they added an elite-scoring winger in Patrick Kane in the draft who is the most talented and creative offensive star in the league. He has a combination of scoring weapons with speed, puck handling, vision and passing.

They put it all together by adding one of the best coaches in the league in Joel Quenneville who is an expert at developing young talent and making brilliant in-game adjustments.

They knew it would be a process, but they continued to add to their base with long-term focus in mind and it paid off in the end with Stanley Cup victories.

If you are just starting to save, it can be tough because there are bills to pay and things to buy and you may not have a lot to start with. But the simple key to building wealth, as mentioned previously is spend less than you make and with that difference, save and invest it.

Before you spend money on more stuff or another toy, make sure you pay yourself first. What does that mean? It means, save before you spend. It goes hand in hand with spend less than you make.

The earlier you start, the more it will pay off in the end because I'm pretty sure you want to retire someday, and it won't come by waiting until the day before and money magically appearing in your account. The Blackhawks didn't just get all their star players at once and win the championship right away. They built through the draft, continually adding pieces and players and it paid off in the end.

What Players Do I Need to Win the Championship? How Much Do I Have to Save For Retirement?

Here's a question people ask a lot: "How much do I need to set aside each month to retire?"

I wish there was an easy answer, but the answer depends on so many variables and a lot of guesses. Just like there is no one-size fits all formula for the exact type of players you need to win a championship, there is not one number or percentage that you need to hit for you to retire.

"Great that really encourages me to save…"

Wait that doesn't mean you just give up. The great news is there are many strategies and ways you can save for retirement.

THE GAME PLAN

In order to retire, you will need to accumulate a pool of capital during your working years that can provide you with a reasonable lifestyle during your retirement years.

"Seems pretty straightforward, but you say there is still no specific formula for this? C'mon man!"

Well it's not as straightforward as it seems. You need to consider the following questions and variables:

- What age will you retire?
- What age will you die?
- What will the tax rates be in your retirement years?
- What will inflation be like?
- How much will health care cost you?
- Will government programs such as Canadian Pension Plan (CPP) be altered before you start to draw from them?
- What rate of return will you earn on your investments over the years?

You see why the how much do I save for retirement question is very tricky? I have no idea what the exact answers to all these questions are and neither does your PhD cousin. Nobody else does either. The best we can do is to make educated forecasts and use software based on actuarial tables and historical data. In the end all we are doing is guessing.

But if you stick to a program geared towards a goal, such as retirement or buying a house, you are setting yourself up for success. As my super smart brother-in-law Ryan

Wagner, MSc & CFA says, "you should be able to live off 2% of your net worth before considering retiring early". That should give at least a benchmark to shoot for at the age you want to "hang up the jersey".

When looking at the 2014 World Series Champion Kansas City Royals, they followed a similar blueprint as the Chicago Blackhawks.

The hardest part is to stick to your plan but you can't back off or you will fall behind. The Royals drafted players with high potential who came up through the minor league system playing together. They added free agent pitchers to the team that over 5 to 6 years became MLB champions.

The process took some time and sometimes fans became impatient but eventually their patience paid off.

Different sport, different needs and goals but they built wisely through the draft and free agent signings.

So back to the original question - how much do I have to save? What do all the experts and financial gurus suggest? They all consistently suggest that we should save between 10 and 15 percent of gross income. Yes, gross income. That is income before things like expenses and taxes.

That does seem like a lot but it is very possible and just by cutting a little back on your spending can increase your ability to save more. I think that when you save more and spend less you will actually be happier in the end. There are many simple things you can do to make yourself an all-star saver. As I'll explain later, make your savings work for you by investing to make sure you reach your goals.

With that, I'll end this chapter with five tips that can help you become a better saver.

5 Tips to Becoming a Better Saver:

1. Cut out convenience

If you're hitting Starbucks every morning, taking Ubers all the time *and* ordering takeout on a regular basis, it can start to add up over time and make a dent in your budget by spending more than your bringing in (hmm sounds like something you read last chapter??). Costs like daily lattes and taking a 5 minute Uber vs. walking can add up big time. So stop buying 5 pairs of basketball shoes, try to limit eating out and stop doing the things that waste money and make life easier but don't add any value. It's easy now but in the long run it's going to make it harder.

2. Pause before checkout

Every time you checkout at the grocery store, or any store, take a look in your cart and find three to five items that you don't need. You will save $5 to $10 every time you shop without using a single coupon. You can apply this tip to online purchases too, where it is painlessly easy to buy a bunch of stuff using Amazon Prime and not notice the amount you've actually spent because you don't physically walk out of a store with 10 bags in your hand. I love Amazon but be smart when shopping online. It's painless for a reason; they're tricking us into getting things we do not need. Think about experiences and not stuff. No matter if you are driving a Ferrari or a civic the road remains the same.

3. Make a list when you shop

Don't go shopping blind. Believe me, I've been there. It's easy to walk around the store and throw in something that of course you'll use ("eventually") but it all adds up. To counter this, make a list of exactly what you need before entering any store. If you're going grocery shopping, my wife and I always make sure we develop our meal plan and ingredients to make sure we only get what we need. Of course you can throw in a box of cookies every once in a while just to keep things interesting...

4. Don't keep up with the Joneses

It's hard to avoid the influence of the Joneses seemingly wealthy lifestyles and it's really hard to escape all the marketers and advertisers who want us to keep up with those people. These people want us to believe that they are well off. However, if you were able to see inside the Joneses' home and bank accounts, you might see a different story. Truth is, many people live beyond their means. In fact, I think many people have more credit card debt than money in their savings account. If your goal is happiness, keeping up with the Joneses is not the way to get there. Having a nice car, a bigger house, a greener lawn or the newest smartphone probably won't make you happy in the long run. Plus overspending on these material things can drag down your financial stability and make you more stressed and unhappy down the road.

For example, you can get quite the immediate rush after a big purchase such as ripping out of the Best Buy parking lot with your new Lamborghini and the emotions that follow after you realize that this new whip actually doesn't get you friends, now you've blown all your savings on the down payment, realize you can't keep up with the financing payments and fall behind on your retirement account savings...

When you make big purchases, examine your motives for buying it and if you really need it. Oh, and next time you see your neighbour roll up in his debt-financed Lambo, don't buy one for yourself, just ask for a ride.

5. Automate Savings and Bill Payments

Automate your bills. Automate your savings. Automate your credit card payments. Then spend whatever is left over. This allows you to avoid unnecessary late fees and save without you even thinking. It is obvious that if you forget to pay your bills you'll rack up late fees, but what about if you forget to save? You don't immediately receive consequences, so you may keep putting it off which puts you further and further behind. So, automate your savings to the amount you need to achieve your goals so you save without even thinking. If you still have money left over after bills, saving and spending there is only one thing left to do. Give yourself a little treat and save more (or take your wife out!).

4. DEBT MANAGEMENT
(The Kentucky Way)

"The key to happiness is low overhead and no debt."
– Lynda Barry

Thanks to my wife, I may now be the Kentucky Wildcats biggest fan. Okay maybe not their biggest fan because Kentucky fans (known as Big Blue Nation) are arguably the most die-hard fans in sports and I don't think I'm worthy to take that title just yet.

Being a part of Big Blue Nation makes you a part of one of the most successful college basketball programs in the NCAA. Kentucky Basketball has a rich history of championships and winning.

Kentucky Basketball teams are successfully built around not only great individual players but also team chemistry and collaboration. These teams know that if something is holding the team back, such as poor attitudes or work ethic, it must be addressed in order for the team to stay successful.

When people think about their net worth, I'm surprised at how many only consider just the assets side of the balance sheet. They could have $1,000,000 in assets but $300,000 in various forms of debt and still think they are a millionaire…Well they have a million dollars in assets, but we are talking "net worth" and technically $300,000 of that is not your money yet, it belongs to whoever you've borrowed from.

Debt is not a fun word to say, hear, or read. It is way more exciting to learn about strategies for saving more and investing right? But most people will carry some kind of debt in their lifetime, so it is an important aspect to address.

THE GAME PLAN

If you're a hockey fan, you know the devastation of being on the power play and seeing your star player miss a wide open one-timer or shot being blocked where the other team takes it the other way and scores a breakaway goal for a 2-goal swing. If you are a basketball fan, especially for the Raptors, you know the pain of seeing a layup blocked by none other than LeBron James and then speeding back the other away for a slam dunk at the other end of the floor for a 4-point swing.

The goal when tackling debt is to be like the opposing team, which makes a comeback after what looked like a sure loss – spending money - into a victory - saving money/paying off and avoiding debt.

As we learned, training the human brain to save is hard. And investing with our emotions, such as fear and greed, affect our investment decisions. The same behaviour can lead to increasing our debt loads as well as borrowing too much.

Try to embed in your head that each day you think of buying something for the sake of buying something is actually a day where you will pay down debt. As soon as you turn the equation around, you will realize how much better it feels to pay down debt than be stuck with a $300 golf driver that you use twice and realize it's not the driver, it's the golfer.

Debt, for the most part, depresses wealth accumulation.

If you have debt, coming up with a strategy to pay down that debt is great for increasing your net worth. If you don't have debt yet but are considering buying houses or cars, weigh the pros and cons before you make big decisions and tie yourself up. If you don't have debt, good for you, continue to rock the savings game for success.

Understanding Acceptable Debt vs. Bad Debt

Too many people don't know the difference between acceptable debt and bad debt. Many people create a debate between good and bad debt, but I don't think there is such thing as "good" debt. There are better kinds of debt, but I don't think that debt is something people crave to have.

The best kind of debt is one that helps you achieve something important like buying a home or getting an education. You don't want to hold onto this debt, but it is acceptable because it will add value in the end.

Real estate is not a great investment on average, but it can be a great asset for you to build equity through a fixed rate mortgage. Housing can be illiquid if you need to sell quickly and pull out your cash. Plus, you don't want to put all of your eggs in one basket, which is the equivalent of putting all your money in one stock.

As long as you have your mortgage balance paid off by the time you retire, this is a perfectly acceptable form of debt.

And if you have to choose between a fixed and adjustable rate mortgages, choose the fixed rate. Don't try and game the system since no one has any way of predicting the coming interest rate environment. And often-adjustable rate mortgages are difficult to understand and cause more uncertainty when planning your future.

Carrying an outstanding debt balance on a line of credit and credit card is bad debt.

You do not want to be carrying bad debt because it comes with costly consequences. It keeps too many people trapped in financial anxiety and powerlessness and feeling like they can never get ahead.

Many people compound these matters by putting bad debt on credit cards, pay minimum payments at a very high rate of interest and take time paying them off. At the same time, they are making accelerated payments on a mortgage that is a low rate of interest and appreciating which doesn't make any sense.

The aim should always be to accumulate the highest net worth at the lowest possible cost. You should get rid of your bad debt first and as fast as you can.

It is tempting to say don't borrow money at all but unfortunately that is difficult advice in the society we live in. Owning a home and even a car would be next to impossible if not for the ability to finance it.

The best advice is to borrow as little as possible as cheaply as possible and repay as quickly as possible. This is especially true for bad debt, which you should try to avoid like the plague.

Change Mindset to Reduce Debt

With our consumer driven society, we are constantly seeing products we should buy and have. It becomes so ingrained in our mindset that it is difficult to get out of.

It's funny because there is no law or rule that says people are supposed to borrow more than they should. It's simply how people are wired. If banks are offering money at a cheap interest rate to live beyond the means, people will take it despite the consequences.

But in order to buy things you can't afford today, you need to pull your spending forward from the future. But by borrowing money now you have created a time at some point in the future that you need to spend less than you make in order to pay it back. That decision is something you can control.

One of the most important things is to control what you can control. You can either buy that second car on a line of credit even though you work only 10 minutes away, or you can take the bus, bike or carpool.

When Kentucky Basketball head coach John Calipari is putting together his team, he is tasked with changing many of his players' tendencies and mindsets in order to achieve success as a team. He asks gifted players (many who were top recruits and stars on their high school teams) to do less than more. Take fewer shots, score fewer points; don't hold possession of the basketball too long.

When Anthony Davis was on Kentucky, Calipari had to beg him to shoot the ball more. He also had other players like Malik Monk, who in high school would put up 40-50 shots a game, become a more efficient scorer by sharing and shooting the right shots that made the team better.

He can control many other things like picking the line-up, making substitutions and deciding what offense and defence to run.

You can control how you spend and where your money goes. You can pick what things you want to put in your starting line-up of life such as a house or new kitchen. You may have debt on these items but you can make the substitutions such as paying off the credit card debt that will make your team better.

Delayed gratification is no fun, but spending now is. However, every purchase you make on credit now means less and less money to spend in the future. This requires a delicate balance between enjoying yourself in the present and being mindful of your future self.

When you realize that not pulling out that extra cash from your line of credit or credit card will actually be better for your "team" (yourself and your family) in the long-run it changes how you manage your money.

Strategies to Get Out of Debt

1. Pay off debt with the highest interest rates first.

Mathematically this strategy makes the most sense because it will save you the most money. If you have $8,000 of credit card debt at 19%, definitely pay down your credit card first before paying down your student loan debt at 5%.

When the Toronto Maple Leafs realized they needed to reshape their organization the smart way, the first thing they did was get rid of high priced players that didn't fit in their success model, that were holding them back from building up assets in other areas.

They shipped out high priced forwards David Clarkson and Phil Kessel as well as defenseman Dion Phaneuf because these players were a high cost to the team that wasn't helping them get better and limited them from adding new pieces to improve the team.

If you are holding credit card debt this is holding you back from building up your investments for your future. And the 19% that credit cards charge is near impossible to beat with your investments so there is no way you should be investing regularly until your credit card balance shows zero. Best advice; never carry a balance on your credit card at the end of the month. Never.

2. Have a plan to get out of debt

Most people think that they will be in debt forever. Don't let that be you and set a roadmap to a date where you will become debt-free. Sports teams such as the Chicago Blackhawks decided that they wanted to no longer be a franchise stuck at the bottom. They made a plan and stuck to it to win championships. At the beginning it will seem impossible but marking checkpoints and small victories will help you get to the end goal.

3. Utilize Automation

If you are having trouble paying off debt, utilize automated reminders (texts, daily Smartphone alerts, emails, etc.) to stay on track. Even better is to create a savings account dedicated specifically for your debt that automatically transfers to your line of credit or credit card to pay them down before you spend any more.

Strategies to not get into Debt

1. **Skip the starter home**

Buying a house is a **huge commitment**, huge price, requires a lot of work and consumes a large part of your budget. There's no reason to rush into buying a house when you're young just because it seems like the next step for being an adult. There's nothing wrong with renting for a few years until you're ready financially to buy a home because housing will likely be your biggest expense item every month. You need to make sure you are able to put a sizable down payment (try to make it more than just the minimum) and still have enough money for your lifestyle needs.

Kind of like when a sports team ties all their money up in one star player thinking that is the next step to building a successful team. However, this doesn't leave much to spend for the rest of the team and build around that player. To be successful you need to be flexible enough to surround your star with pieces like a solid goalie or star defensemen.

If you tie up all your money in a house you are limited in how you can build a great financial team around it with other essential pieces such as retirement savings, emergency fund and education funds. Because once your money is tied up in a house and you run short for a month, you can't just get it back immediately. Owning a home is expensive. Beyond your mortgage and interest payments there's upkeep, property taxes, furniture & decorations and the cost of home improvements.

I don't know everyone's personal situation so it's not fair to make a blanket statement on this topic. Buying a home is always situation dependent. The numbers can change depending on your down payment, geography, local market conditions, current financial situation and future plans. The house will be the biggest thing you buy in your life so make sure you are prepared to make it worth it.

2. Skip the new car

A new car is a depreciating asset. If you can't save money, you have no business buying a new vehicle. Besides the initial cost of a car, you also have to pay expensive ongoing costs such as car insurance, maintenance, fuel, parking tickets. When you add everything up, it can be shocking at how much it really costs you to own a car!

There are a lot of reasons why we take on debt; some are reasonable and acceptable, some are not. For the most part, debt is a burden that drags down our net worth and is a struggle psychologically. There's something amazing about no longer being indebted to anyone or organization. You feel freer. There is so much satisfaction when you simplify your life with one less recurring bill payment.

5. SURVIVING COLLEGE YEARS (ROOKIE OF THE YEAR)

"Get the fundamentals down and the level of everything you do will rise."
-Michael Jordan

Being a rookie in professional sports is a giant leap, not only competition but also lifestyle change. There are so many things to think about such as working on your game in practice, competing night in and night out against the world's best and trying to locate the closest Chick-Fil-A in every city.

At such a young age, getting that first big-league contract and seeing all the bright lights bring on euphoria that nothing can go wrong and can cause you to be naive to the little things. It may seem impossible for these million-dollar athletes to go broke but, *Sports Illustrated* found that after two years of retirement, 78 percent of NFL players are bankrupt or under financial stress (Torre, 2009).

Former NBA No. 1 draft pick Joe Smith earned $61 million over his 16-year career. That's more money than most people see in a lifetime. Yet only six years from being retired, he is living paycheck to paycheck and owes $157,000 in debt. Thanks to reckless spending, bad investments and a costly divorce, Smith found that his fortune had been completely wiped out (Torre, 2009).

Crazy. If you don't watch where your money goes, you won't know what to change or do when it runs low.

This can be the same kind of feeling for students starting college or university. They experience a lot of firsts, including managing a budget. The temptation to spend is everywhere. Waiting until after college to take control of your finances could cost you. And just like starting that New Year's fitness program or starting that 40-page thesis paper, getting started is half the battle.

When you start university, college or any post-secondary program as well as putting together your finances, you will begin to hear and learn a lot of new things from many different sources. As you learn throughout this stage of life, you need to make sure sources are credible and they fit with your idea or situation or else it won't resonate with you.

Back Up Your Sources (and your bracket)

March Madness for NCAA College Basketball has to be the greatest tournament in all of sports. Every game is do or die between the best basketball programs in the country who have played their hearts out all year to get into this tournament. The games are intense; back and forth and always feature amazing matchups with some thrilling buzzer beaters.

Every year features surprising upsets at every turn. I'm sure there are many people out there who have filled out brackets that have gotten absolutely crushed (I am one of them). Cinderella stories usually make an appearance every year taking everyone by surprise.

Take 2018's No. 16 seed UMBC taking down the number one team in the country Virginia in the first round. Before that game, no 16 seed had ever, in the history of the tournament, taken down a 1 seed. But crazy things happen in sports and like the investment saying goes, past performances don't mean future results. I bet zero people saw UMBC's epic win coming (I mean who had even heard of them?) and they blew up everyone's brackets.

There are also the times when your bracket is busted because you just made bad picks (picking the teams with the best mascots usually does not work).

The weekend before the tournament starts, my family and I start to watch the March Madness Bracketology specials 24/7 and listen to the college basketball analysts looking for information, news and predictions for the tournament. These are the experts that will help us create the perfect tournament bracket and win the million-dollar prize from Warren Buffett. We think these analysts' predictions will give us the answers we need for our own brackets.

Truth is they know nothing how the tournament will play out. Nobody does. And this happens every year. They don't hold the crystal ball and we don't know the motivation these guys have for making their predictions. A lot of the time these analysts are just trying to make interesting television. So that's why they pick some upsets and some stories for people to buy into. Then people choose the chosen upsets for their bracket, lose their family pool and then blame ESPN.

This same situation plays out on business news channels every day. There's a lot of air time to fill throughout the day so since boring, simple long-term advice that works won't make for good TV, they fill the screens with stories on why the market is behaving a certain way, short-term economic data points, hot stock picks, and mixing up the conversation by playing some devil's advocate.

And while people need good advice, what they want is advice that sounds good.

And I'm not saying that these people don't know what they are talking about; I just don't think that the news channel is where you should be getting your sole financial advice. At the end of the day, these people don't know your specific personal situation, your risk profile or time horizon and your different goals.

So while it can be entertaining to watch the people argue over different stock picks, it won't do much for your financial well being. In fact, if you take the advice from the news then you will probably end up much like your March madness bracket. You may as well flip a coin.

You are better off not watching the day-to-day news and staying disciplined to your plan.

Wall Street Journal columnist Jason Zweig pointed to brilliant research by psychologist Paul Andreassen in an article that people who receive frequent news updates on their investments earn lower returns than those who get no news (Zweig, 2015). Reason being: they become more inclined to make emotional and irrational decisions that can detriment their long-term returns.

"Not many people care to admit that they spend their careers being part of the problem instead of trying to be part of the solution." (Zweig, 2015)

So, whether you're learning at school, writing a paper, or getting investment advice, you must always consider the source whether it's from the Business Network, your professor or your next-door neighbour. Figure out what incentive they have for giving you that hot stock tip or predicting a 20% drop in stocks over the next 12 months. Make sure you do your own research when making a decision and that it fits into your investment plan.

Developing a Plan for your College Prospect - Teams point of view - develop prospect

It is proven in sports time and time again that when teams rush the development of their prospects, they don't get the full value out of those players. There are multiple examples of a team drafting a player high with potential and throwing them into the league when they may not be ready which erodes their confidence and makes it even tougher for the players to break in.

In the NHL, the Detroit Red Wings and Winnipeg Jets are two teams that have taken their time to develop players properly and have turned into powerhouse teams.

"Your mother and I need more time to save for your college education. We'd like you to go back to Kindergarten and start over."

THE GAME PLAN

Detroit would always take their time with bringing players up, despite fans wanting to see their top prospects. Pavel Datsyuk and Henrik Zetterberg learned the game in the minor league system and were slowly brought into bigger roles once they played the way the team expected them to play - strong two way hockey. They then became the best two-way players in the league.

Winnipeg was up and coming with high draft picks such as Mark Scheifele and Nikolaj Ehlers. They both showed flashes of brilliance in their first couple games with the club but despite their scoring and the fans wanting them to stay, the Jets sent them down to continue to develop them. Fast-forward and they are both pillars on a Jets team that is one of the best in the league.

It takes time and it takes a plan to get you where you want to go. If you aimlessly work at something, you will never hit the mark needed to be successful. That is why it is so important to plan your finances the same way, especially with funding your children's education.

In developing a college funding plan, most people don't know or don't fully use the tools at their disposal and end up leaving their college planning too late, which doesn't give their children (their top prospects) the best chance to succeed.

Paying for college is a big expense. The high (and rising) cost of tuition and the amount of student loans that younger generations are taking with them upon graduation makes this is an important topic for parents to consider. In fact, if a family has two or more children, their total college expenses could end up being more than their mortgage.

And the earlier you start saving the less you have to save overall (the magic of compound interest). Teachers, of all people, know there is no shortcut to learning something well (a semester can not be learned in a day).

By starting early you give yourself almost 20 years to save and invest. Small amounts of money saved over that period of time can really start to add up. If you start when your child is age 0, save $100 a month, and are able to earn 5% on your money, you would end up with over $40,000 after 20 years.

The RESP

An RESP is the best option for saving for your child's education and to not have them work 30 hours/week at McDonald's while trying to study during school. Having an RESP is like having a world-class training facility for your top prospects to work on their skill development.

One of the main benefits of an RESP is that the government will match a certain amount of the money that is contributed into an account. Sounds great but of course, being the government, the rules get a little complicated. Here's the basic rundown:

The Canadian Education Savings Grant (CESG) matches 20% of the amount you contribute to your RESP. You will only get the government match on a max of $2,500 per child per year, but the maximum grant annually per child is $500. Even if you contribute $5,000 per child you will just get the maximum $500. However, you can do this annually until you've received $7200 in government funds for each child which is the lifetime limit.

Here is the tax-situation. While the money is in the account, all gains will remain tax-free (yes, TAX FREE). When a student withdraws the money to pay for school, he or she will owe tax only on the interest, dividends, and capital gains, and on the money supplied by the government. But the money he or she or his or her family originally contributed will not be taxed, since that money was taxed already. This is one of the best benefits the government provides so take advantage.

Rookie of the Year

Being a student is tough. Long nights studying, partying, living away from home and managing your finances so it doesn't hurt you down the road. When you graduate it is a great accomplishment and on the right track for a successful career. However, being set back by your financial situation can hinder you for many years.

Luckily, there are many simple strategies students can do that still allow you to have the best college experience while being smart while doing it.

Here are eight student financial tips to help them manage their finances, get good value and minimize reckless spending.

1. **Create (and stick to) a budget**

Create a realistic budget that also gives you a little money for fun… yes, fun! Review it each month to make sure you stay on track and have time to adjust it as needed. To make it easier - use a budgeting app on your phone, which helps you easily create and stick to a budget.

2. Be careful with credit

Remember that a credit card doesn't equal free money. If you can handle a credit card, start with a $1,000-limit card that offers points or other rewards and pay your balance monthly. It's not worth it to strap yourself with a high-interest, annual-fee credit card that you don't need.

3. Save early and often

While investing in your 20's may sound boring, starting young is easily the best way to get ahead. It's easy to think you have all kinds of time to get your financial life together so what difference will it make if you put off investing for a while? Unfortunately, waiting can make a world of difference.

Some athletes start on successful paths early on in their careers. For example, 2014 Canadian Olympic gold medallist Dara Howell won the first ever-Olympic gold medal awarded in ski slopestyle when she was still a teenager. Dara started skiing at 18 months old and continued to slowly work on the slopes to develop technique and skills that would bode her well in the future. Even after she won the gold medal at the Olympics, she continued to persevere to always keep pushing forward towards her goals. When you invest it isn't a one and done mentality. Dara continued to invest into her skiing career even after her gold medal just like investors continue to save and invest after a big gain.

Same habits can transfer over to saving. Let's say you invest $300 per month starting at age 20 and don't stop until you're 60-years-old. If you managed an 8 percent return during that time, you would have more than $1 million dollars at age 60. Now let's say you waited until you were 30 to get started. By the time you reached 60-years-old, you would only have $440,445 in your account. Those first ten years you missed out on would cost you more than $550,000 in returns – less than half of what you could have if you started earlier! This is the magic of compound interest.

4. Take advantage of student perks

College students should become masters at exploring the ways their educational status can save them money. Vendors, local venues, restaurants, events and services near college campuses often offer student discounts that could save big money throughout your degree. And by looking for discounts, students learn the value of hunting down great deals.

5. Buy used wherever possible

Items like furniture, pots, pans and small appliances are easy to find on Kijiji and some stores have used sections. If you're looking for something in particular, post an ad or ask your personal network.

6. Split the cost of a textbook with a classmate

Depending on the course, students can save hundreds of dollars each semester by buying used textbooks or sharing the cost of new ones with a classmate. There have been many courses that I've taken where you can buy an online textbook but share the book and the cost amongst other students. Depending on how many people you get to share you can have the textbook for like $5.

7. Learn to cook

Constantly buying food at restaurants is expensive on a student budget. Parents can help by sharing a few tried and true recipes before students go off to university.

8. Have Fun
There are lots of ways to have a good time in college without breaking the bank.

6. SUPER BOWL INVESTING

"Not investing is a sure-fire way to fail to accumulate the wealth necessary to ensure a sound financial future."
- John C. Bogle

Super Bowl 52 featured a matchup between the powerhouse New England Patriots and the Philadelphia Eagles. The Patriots dynasty was looking to win their second straight Super Bowl and their sixth in 17 years, which would have been unprecedented.

Tom Brady passed for a Super Bowl record 505 yards and tossed three touchdowns (Reyes, 2018). His offense never punted. He was sacked just once, but that one sack led to a costly fumble on the plus side of the two-minute warning. If he could have avoided Brandon Graham and gotten that pass off with 2:14 left in the game, the Patriots would have had a much better chance at their second straight Super Bowl comeback.

"I knew they had a good rush," Brady said. "They made a good play. They made a good play at the right time. They made *one* good play at the right time." (Birch, 2018)

Sometimes you can have the best team or the best portfolio in the world but when you are investing in the market, there is always the risk of a loss.

If there was a way to predict the markets then everyone would know what to do. Just like if everyone was as good as the Golden State Warriors or the New England Patriots, then they wouldn't be known as being such great teams. But even those great teams eventually lose. There will always be winners and losers - the market is a zero sum game (Gray, 2017).

Long term investing is the only reason you should invest and the most proven way to get results. Going back to the New England Patriots, they have had the same quarterback and coach for the last 17 years. The results have been better than any other team in the NFL. They have recorded the most wins and Super Bowls during that time by sticking to their process through the highs and lows. No they don't win every year, just like in investing you won't get a return of 20% every year. There will be times where you will lose but the biggest thing is to not run from those losses but hold on and press forward during the rough stretches.

Tom Brady's quote after their Super Bowl 52 loss can be a huge reminder for investors "If you're not in the game, you don't have a chance to win. If you want to be world champs you need to be in this game" (Fansided Staff, 2018). You can parallel this to investors the same way by saying 'If you're not investing in the market, you don't have a chance to make a return on your money. If you want to have a winning portfolio you need to be invested and stick with it over the long term.' The Patriots lost the game but if they weren't in the game they wouldn't have even had the chance to win. Every other team in the league was out sitting on the sidelines with 0% chance to win that game.

Many people are sitting on the sidelines with cash making little to no money at all. If you are holding money on the sidelines of the market, you are missing out on opportunity to gain and use the power of compounding and time value of money to help provide yourself with a better financial future. In fact, if you are holding money in cash then you are actually losing purchasing power when you take inflation into effect.

Don't get me wrong; putting money in a savings account is great. In fact, that act of saving is awesome and you shouldn't stop.

When you put money into your savings account you'll feel a rush of joy after that deposit — "Look at that, it's all there. I didn't use it to buy a whole new set of golf clubs!" But then you start to see what your peers are earning by investing their money in growth portfolios with an average rate of return of 6% annually. Suddenly 1% (that's about as well as you could do in a high interest savings account right now) won't feel so great. Your level of joy will drop even further when you realize that, since inflation is about 2%, you'll actually be *losing* money by keeping it in a "high-interest" savings account.

There are times where you need to set aside cash such as an emergency fund for rainy day moments but if you are not investing for your future, retirement, house, anything you dream of, it is a very hard thing to do unless you are in the market.

Overcoming the fear of investing

People need to reshape their thinking on investing. The best time to invest in stocks in when they are cheap, (when the market drops) however most people freak out when the market goes down and don't want to invest. They need to think as if they are going shopping at a mall.

When you go to the mall there are hundreds of stores and if you see a big sale at some stores, you wouldn't run away, instead you would go buy something because why wouldn't you buy something on sale instead of at full price. It doesn't make sense to buy something at full or even overprice when you can buy it on sale.

Same concept applies for stocks. The market will have its ups and downs. Sometimes it can go down a lot at once such as a correction, world events like the Corona Virus or even recession. When this happens, most people act irrationally (which makes sense because portfolio is going down). They sell hoping to avoid losses or wait until the market goes back up and "settles down".

But they should drop back to the shopping mall mindset. Why would I wait for a sale to end at a store allowing prices to increase and then buy at these more expensive prices? It doesn't make sense.

Also, sometimes after a sale, they put the price up to an even higher price than before. In the stock market, the biggest gains usually come right after a drop in the market. You don't want to be jumping in and out of the market especially when you don't know what will likely happen next.

It is easy to say buy low, sell high but reality is that it is very tough mentally and behaviour to follow that rule. Would you have been able to buy at the bottom of the market in the 2008 financial crisis when everyone was predicting a double dip recession during the market's snapback rally?

It is very detrimental to your portfolios long-term returns to be in and out of the market. In other words, hold on and ride the train back up.

Then there are people who keep their cash on the sidelines waiting for that sale price but you never know when it's going to go on sale. And if you wait for a year from now, prices go up with inflation and that shirt you wanted for $29.95 is now $34.95.

Time value of money and businesses want to keep making more money so the best thing you can do is continue to invest, don't run away when things "go on sale", and follow your plan.

Every season has its ups and downs

Every sport season has its ups and downs, whether it be winning streaks or losing streaks, awards or injuries, team success or team chemistry problems. But teams continue to play throughout the season just like businesses operate throughout the year and go through cycles of ups and downs.

The stock market is volatile and always changing. If you are going to invest that is something you need to know and embrace, which also means suffering through uncomfortable times. But that is the secret for what makes a great investor and a great team. Suffering through uncomfortable times helps produce good results.

That's why discipline and patience is mentioned so often in investing and sports because that is the key to success.

Even though the Chicago Bulls in the 80's had the greatest basketball player on the planet in Michael Jordan, they didn't win every single game during all those seasons.

It's a long season where the team faced injuries and bouts against tough physical teams. That only made them stronger and more prepared for the playoffs where they went onto win 6 championships.

Investing for the long-term will come with short-term volatility but when you stick to the process and learn from your mistakes, your portfolio and finances will become championship worthy.

When you understand that volatility and market declines are a part of investing in the market you don't panic when market drops come and go. In fact, you're more prepared when you already expect it to happen. A great quote from one of the best investors Peter Lynch describes market volatility perfectly:

"You get recessions, you have stock market declines. If you don't understand that's going to happen, then you're not ready — you won't do well in the markets. If you go to Minnesota in January, you should know that it's going to be cold. You don't panic when the thermometer falls below zero."

The stock market does not go up every single day. It is volatile so you shouldn't panic when it goes down. That's what happens. Investing is rarely a stroll through the park. You never know what might happen next. Embracing that reality is never easy, but it's important to long-term success.

Stock Picking – Hail Mary and Drive for Show, Putt for Dough

THE GAME PLAN

How many times has the power of slow and steady progress been the best option? Slow and steady usually comes out on top - be it at the gym, in school or in your career. Why, then, do we expect it to be different with investing? A slow, steady and disciplined approach will go a lot farther over the long haul than going for the 'Hail Mary' last-minute plays.

A Hail Mary is usually a last ditch effort for a football team to try and score a touchdown. It is a high-risk high reward play but the reward rarely pays out. You would think it's silly if a team was throwing a Hail Mary every single play. The chances of success are slim. The same goes for people trying to pick certain stocks to try and beat the market. Even worse is doing a Hail Mary where you throw all your money into one stock thinking that will be the path to the lottery. That involves a large amount of risk that has little chance of payoff.

Another example is in golf where someone pulls out their driver and tries to rip it down the course swinging as hard as they can. That looks good and all but the drive is worthless if the golfer takes 3 putts to get the ball in the hole every time. The saying goes 'drive for show, putt for dough' and that is the truth.

It's useless to be crushing your tee shots while three-putting every green. Investors are drawn to glamour stocks because the payoffs can be huge. But while they have great possibilities, they also have bad probabilities.

It is incredibly hard to beat the market yet people continue to try and pick stocks that can beat the market.

THE GAME PLAN

When 90% of professional investors, with their PhD's and powerful computers and multimillion-dollar research budgets, can't beat the market, why should you believe anyone who says you can do it by day trading?

No one can predict where the markets are going to go in the short or even immediate term. Warren Buffett himself states,

"I can't predict the short-term movements of the stock market. I haven't the faintest idea as to whether stocks will be higher or lower a month — or a year — from now."

Stock investing is not easy, but don't try to make it more complicated than it has to be. The best thing to do is invest in low-cost, diversified funds that own the entire market and have an investment plan in advance that you will stick to through the good times and the bad. While that's not the coolest thing to talk about at your work party, by having a system in place you will know what to do no matter what the current market conditions.

7. COMPOUNDING (LIKE AUSTON MATTHEWS)

"Compound interest is the eighth wonder of the world. He who understands it earns it…he who doesn't…pays it."
- Albert Einstein

One of the common objections people have to building an investment portfolio is that they feel they "aren't wealthy enough" to start thinking about investing their money. I believe that at any stage of your life and regardless of your income, you can start to invest for future wealth.

Compound interest is a really good way to watch your money grow while doing nothing. You work hard for your money so shouldn't it work just as hard for you?

In simple terms, compound interest is the principle by which the interest you earn also earns interest, and the interest on that interest earns interest, and so on and so on. The larger your balance gets, the bigger those interest numbers become. It's like a team that gets on a winning streak, slowly picking up speed and size at first, but really takes off over the long run as wins build on top of wins.

The earlier you start saving using a compound interest account, the more advantage you get. As the balance gets bigger, so does the benefit of compounding.

If you're a young person in their early 20's, holding 80% of your investments in cash – and you're not on the verge of buying a home or paying off the entirety of your student debt – you are wasting the most precious resource known to investors everywhere: Time.

When it comes to compounding, time is more valuable than any analysis, research, investing tools or trading service. You can be the most boring investor on earth and, with enough time spread out before you, can outperform virtually anyone.

The biggest asset most investors have is time

You may have heard of a really smart dude named Albert Einstein who called compound interest the most powerful force in the universe. If a really smart guy like Einstein thinks it's so great, how come so many people don't take advantage of this world wonder? There are two main reasons.

One, most people just don't understand how it works. For example, 10% growth for 25 years is not 250%, it's 985%! The second reason why many fail to take advantage of compounding is because it takes time. Like, a really long time. Buffett has been rich forever, but 99% of his net worth was earned after his 52nd birthday (Cardone, 2018). That takes lots and lots of patience and discipline.

When talking about compounding and the benefit of starting earlier, I put it in a simple hockey example between two players.

Let's say there is a NHL hockey player (Auston Matthews) who is very aware about the magic of compounding and time. He decides to start saving for retirement as soon as he makes the Toronto Maple Leafs at age 20. Matthews then saves $500 a month into his retirement account until age 35. At this point, Matthews stops saving and just let's compound interest work in his favour. After a long career playing in the NHL and post career broadcasting jobs, Matthews officially retires at age 65. Assuming a 7% annual rate of return he will retire with $1,184,101 even though he only contributed $90,000 total into his account.

Another NHL player (Patrik Laine) decides to wait until he is 35 to start saving. He saves the same $500 a month that Auston Matthews did but he actually continues to save that amount right up until the day he retires. His total amount contributed to his account over those 30 years would be $180,000. Assuming he also earns an annual return of 7% on his funds he will end up with $584,726 when he retires. The chart below shows the story:

	Auston Matthews	Patrik Laine
Monthly Savings	$500	$500
Annual return	7%	7%
Total Contributions	$90,000	$180,000
Years of Saving	15	30
Ending Balance Age 65	$1,184,101	$584,726

Even though Patrik Laine contributed 2x as much money as Auston Matthews did, he actually ends up with half the amount that Matthews has at retirement. The reason for this is compound interest. As I explained before, compounding with time is like a giant snowball effect — the longer the hill is, the bigger the snowball can get. Compound interest means that you continually earn interest on top of your principal + interest which snowballs until you have a runaway avalanche working in your favour.

Auston Matthews' 10-year head start on Laine gave himself more than double his ending balance. Time is by far the biggest advantage to have in investing because of compounding. Imagine how different your lifestyle would be in your later years when you have twice the amount of money in the bank. You would have the flexibility to maybe travel more, maybe try starting your own business, being able to help out your kids or others. Just by Auston Matthews starting to invest 10 years earlier, he didn't have to work as hard later on to save.

Just for fun, let's assume Auston Matthews doesn't stop saving at age 35. Instead, he continues saving the same amount his entire career after playing in the NHL and until he retires at age 65. With the same assumptions, Matthews now has over $1.7 million at retirement.

Sidney Crosby - Coffee Connoisseur

How much do you think you spend daily on coffee? $4? $6? $10? Are you on a first-name basis with your Starbucks barista or Tim Horton's roaster? How much do you think you would have, if you had one less cup a day, used the power of compounding and invested the money you saved? Let's look at another compounding example where hypothetically hockey star and Tim Horton's ambassador Sidney Crosby aka "Sid the Kid" is a notorious coffee connoisseur.

THE GAME PLAN

Let's say Crosby buys two cups of coffee a day at $2 each before he heads to the rink. What would happen if he cut his coffee consumption in half, only bought one coffee and invested the savings?

Well, history shows us that the average annual rate of return of the stock market has been around 6% after inflation. So if Crosby invested that $2 instead of buying coffee, his $2 would be worth $20.57 in 40 years.

If he invested a months worth of saved $2 coffee, he would have around $620 in profit each year.

And what would happen if Sidney Crosby, "Golden Goal scorer", 3-time Stanley Cup Champion, Pittsburgh Penguins legend turned intelligent investor invested his $2 coffee savings for the rest of his playing career and post NHL weatherman career? He would have One Hundred and Eighty Thousand Dollars! All from just saving $2 daily for 46 years.

Once again the power of compounding shows that even small amounts and a long time horizon creates incredible results. It is never too small to start investing!

Stacking the Odds in your favour

1. Starting to invest earlier increases the length of the investment period, giving your initial investment a greater time to compound and grow.
2. Even if you don't think you have enough money to start investing, the smallest amounts can grow into a substantial amount if invested wisely and given enough time.

3. Just changing your spending habits ever so slightly (just by cutting out small avoidable expenses) can bring about a huge positive benefit for your finances in the long run.
4. A RRSP is a great way to juice your returns. If you work at an employee who does RRSP matching - take advantage of that free money. You can literally double your money with an employer RRSP match. Using round numbers as an example, an employee earning $100,000 contributing 5% can sock away $5,000 and get a 100% return on their money if the employer matches that contribution. Oh yea, those tax deferrals aren't bad either.
5. Saving more money can offset lower returns because you're compounding on top of compounding. Starting with zero dollars and investing for 20 years while earning 4% and raising your contribution by 10% each year will leave you $100,000 richer in year 20 than earning 6% and raising your contribution by only 5%.

8. ASSET ALLOCATION/DIVERSIFY (TEAM WORLD)

"Stock picking is for fun. Asset allocation is for making money over the long haul."
– Barry Ritholtz

THE GAME PLAN

When you look at the sports teams that win championships, they usually gather players from all parts of the world and specialists at different positions that put together a solid team in all areas. If you have a basketball team with just 6-foot point guards going up against NBA teams with an "average" height of around 6-foot 7 inches, I'm sorry but you aren't going to win many games. You need to diversify. When thinking about investing and constructing your portfolio one of the most fundamental (if not the most fundamental) rules of investing is the importance of having a well-diversified portfolio.

You have probably heard this concept before: "make sure you diversify." But what does that really mean and why does it matter? Isn't the whole point of investing trying and maximize the highest return possible? I mean, how else are you going to afford that beach house on the ocean you've been dreaming about?

The answer to both these questions is yes and no. Of course we want to make as much money as possible when we invest, but at what cost? How much risk are we willing to take? The more aggressive (the more risk we take on) there is an increased chance of losing that capital you worked so hard for.

The secret here is diversification. Also known as asset allocation. Asset allocation is the way you split your funds into different asset classes (stocks, bonds, cash, etc.). It is one of the most important decisions that you can make with your investments. The reason you diversify and allocate to different securities that do different things in order to spread the risk out.

With me so far? Great. Here is a golf example.

Drive for show, Putt for Dough

Golfers carry many different clubs in their bag. Typically, they have a driver, some fairway woods, irons, wedges and a putter. Each club is designed for different shots in your game. When you are on the tee and need distance, you hit with your driver because it goes the farthest. When you are on the green you would use a putter because it is the most precise at getting that little white ball into the little hole.

Without that mix of different clubs, you most likely won't play your best because you then wouldn't be prepared for the different types of shots that come your way. Don't believe me? Try playing 18 holes with just a sand wedge and let me know how you shoot.

Think of your golf clubs as different asset classes. Your different asset classes are used for different scenarios in investing.

Stocks: Equity in companies, usually owned for growth
Bonds: Corporate and government debt, own for income and protection against a crisis
Hard Assets: Real Estate and commodities, own for inflation protection and in some real estate, income as well
Cash: Used for new investment opportunities and safety in a crisis

Globetrotting Penguins

When your asset allocation in stocks, bonds, hard assets and cash should also be diversified geographically for increased opportunity and spreading the risk.

The 2016-17 Pittsburgh Penguins became the first NHL team since 1997 to repeat as back-to-back Stanley Cup Champions for the best hockey team in the world. They didn't get it done with just one player obviously. Yes, they have a once-in-a-generation talent in Sidney Crosby, but more importantly, they had specific pieces on a team that were different styles, from different countries, and different roles but they all complimented each other so well.

They had skilled scorers in Phil Kessel and Evgeni Malkin. They had reliable veterans that stepped up in key situations with face-off specialist Matt Cullen and grinder Patrik Hornquist; mobile and stay-at-home defenseman in Oli Maata and Kris Letang. And they had a steady goalie to keep the net safe in Matt Murray. They had a full roster of players, from different countries and different roles, but the point here is simple: they are Stanley Cup Champions because each individual on the team had a specific job to do, and when they all came together, they covered off their weak areas and used their strengths creating a winning formula.

Building your investment portfolio is not too different from creating a successful sports team. Just like you can't have a team full of Sidney Crosby's, you can't have a portfolio full of Amazon's and Apples (recent performance aside). I mean if Sidney Crosby was playing all the roles like score, play defence, kill penalties and play goalie, I don't think they would be successful. What you can do is put together a roster of other securities that are meant to do things well like generate income such as bonds or dividend paying stocks or add long-term growth in value or growth stocks.

It is also important to gather these various forms of securities from different countries and regions around the world such as Europe, U.S, Asia, Australia to go with Canadian securities. If you only had some stocks from Canada, you're missing out on 98% of the world's economy. You can see in the chart below that Canada's stock market represents barely 3% of the world's market - with the U.S holding over 50%.

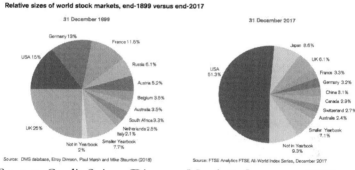

Source: Credit Suisse (Dimson, Marsh & Staunton, 2018)

If Canada's market would falter, you would go down with it because you hold all your risk in that one region. When combining your mix of securities properly in a portfolio across different countries and regions, you get access to more opportunities while lowering your risk - which can be game changing. This "diversification theory" is based on Nobel-prize winning logic from someone who was way smarter than me. If you don't believe me just Google "The Efficient Frontier".

Simplicity beats flashy

Adding the NBA as a diversification example, in the 2011 NBA Finals, the Dallas Mavericks came in as huge underdogs to the favoured Miami Heat who had created what the NBA now calls "the big three" of LeBron James, Dwyane Wade and Chris Bosh. This finals series, at least in this financial planner's mind, show an obvious investment lesson when comparing these two teams.

The Mavericks strategically built a full team of players into a smoothly functioning, integrated system. Their deep and diversified bench gave them flexibility and more steady performance.

In contrast, the Miami Heat led with the flash of their "big three" names who had confidence that they were going to win the title. This strategy left them particularly vulnerable when any one of the three key players had a bad day or got injured.

This raises the question to investors as to how many have been fooled by the promise and lure of a single "hot" investment, the promise of big riches from a single out-sized bet, only to lose their hopes and dreams on that bet, and fail to win the biggest prize of all, long-term financial well-being?

The 2011 NBA Champion Mavericks offer a great reminder that you should avoid the hot news trends and follow the winning formula of diversifying your assets in low-cost ways to offer the greatest rewards over the long term.

How to choose the right Asset Allocation

While you don't want to fully rely on history, by looking at the historical performance of certain asset allocation strategies you can determine how the losses and gains over these cycles would have made you feel. This is called stress-testing your portfolio. You can then see how your emotions and investment decisions would react if similar circumstances arise in the future. There are many online investor profile questionnaires you can take to find out what your risk tolerance is.

Some investors like to take on more risk just like athletes and go for the deep pass, the long drive or long three pointer while others are more comfortable with handing off the ball to the running back, going for the layup or slam dunk.

For investors under the age of 45, you have a long time until retirement and can usually make up for short-term volatility in the stock market while still getting the long-term returns that you need. In this case having a portfolio made up of 80-90% stocks and 10-20% in bonds is an ideal mix if your tolerance for risk allows it.

Someone that is approaching or in retirement or even someone who is buying a house in less than 5 years is more likely to have a 50/50 mix of stocks and bonds or as low as 20-30% in stocks in their portfolio because they have current and future spending needs and must draw down their investment funds for that spending. Having a higher weighting in bonds and a lower weighting in stocks has, in the past, lowered the volatility in your portfolio while also providing some downside protection against large losses.

Remember that the goal is not to have the asset allocation that will outperform all others. No one knows what that will be going forward. You want to choose the one that has worked well over various scenarios and help you achieve your goals while not stressing over your portfolio.

Invest like the best

Investing guru David F. Swensen has been the Chief Investment Officer for Yale University's endowment since 1988 and is considered one of the greatest investors of our time. His simple advice to investors is don't try anything fancy. Stick to a simple diversified portfolio and rebalance periodically to keep your asset allocations in line with your long-term goals.

"Don't be distracted by market forecasts, for every smart person on one side of the question, there is another smart person on the other side." Stick to your long-term asset allocation — even when the markets are in tumult (Fabrikant, 2008).

Remember to diversify next time you review or construct your portfolio. Make sure you gather the different pieces you need to get you to your goals and don't overlook those less exciting securities. Having a well diverse team is often what separates true champions from second place.

"I retire on Friday and I haven't saved a dime. Here's your chance to become a legend!"

9. HALFTIME
(WHAT TO DO IF YOU HAVEN'T SAVED EARLIER)

"Yesterday's home runs don't win today's games."
- Babe Ruth

THE GAME PLAN

So most of what you've read right now has largely been with the assumption that you are in your early 20's and early in your career and that if you start saving in your younger years you should end up with a healthy amount of savings when you retire.

Now let's say you wait until you're 35 to start saving (maybe paying off debt has held you back), or you're 45 and have saved but not enough and are behind your nest egg goal? Life can get in the way sometimes.

But good news! All is not lost if you haven't started saving yet. In fact it is never too late to start. You will just have to do one thing to make up for your shortfall in the coming years:

Increase the amount you save.

Yeah, you could also try and outsmart the markets, outperform all the experts and become the next Warren Buffett. Or there's that Bitcoin thing. Or the lottery. But all those options are just another form of gambling, incredibly risky and you should not gamble with your retirement money.

So you're probably now thinking, "hmm so I actually do have to buckle down and work harder at this savings thing."

Exactly. And that's the mindset you need to have. Buckle down and work hard to come back because you are never out of it.

THE GAME PLAN

And the great thing with sports is there are tons of comeback stories you can draw on and relate to for inspiration.

There's obviously Rocky Balboa getting pummelled by Ivan Drago before rallying to knock out the Russian boxer on enemy ground. But let's look at some real life examples.

The 1980 Olympics featured what is now known as "The Miracle on Ice" where the U.S hockey team won over the long dominant and heavily favoured Soviet Union. The U.S team was composed of college and amateur players whereas the Soviets were well developed who had won the gold in the past four Olympics. Right before the Olympics the Soviets had beaten the U.S in an exhibition match 10-3 so the odds were very slim. But the U.S dug in, worked harder than the Soviets and made the impossible possible! With ten minutes left in the game and the game tied 3-3, Mike Eruzione scored the famous fourth and winning goal to win 4-3.

There's the 2016 Chicago Cubs comeback from 3-1 to beat the Cleveland Indians to win their first World Series in 108 years. The Cubs had one of the best teams in baseball all year but had to rise to the occasion to make their championship dream a reality. The Cubs battled back to force game 7 and shot out to a four-run lead. They then blew that lead and it went into extra innings where they had to come back again to shock the baseball world for the championship.

Also in 2016, the city of Cleveland was on the other side of the equation when the Cavaliers became the first NBA team to comeback from 3-1 in the Finals to win and end Cleveland's 52-year drought without a major sports title. They took down a Golden State Warriors team that was considered one of the best teams of all time. When they were up 3-1 people were already crowning the Warriors champs since teams leading 3-1 were 32-0 all time. The Cavaliers dug in and their best players LeBron James and Kyrie Irving took control in their own hands including a chase down block by LeBron on Andre Iguodala in Game 7 of the finals. They knew the odds were stacked against them but they kept pushing and received a championship result.

Start Now!!

All these examples go on to show that it never too late. Start the comeback now!

If you start at age 40 (assuming a 7% return) and save $750 a month you can still retire at age 65 with $607,553. Or if you save $1,000 a month at age 50 you would have $316,962 at 65. Your increased contributions can make up for some of the lost time.

Another example would be between two young baseball stars, let's say Bryce Harper and Mike Trout. They both start their careers at age 20. Bryce gets off to a great start and hits 20 home runs for his first 10 seasons. He then changes his swing for a bit more power now and improves to hit 40 home runs in each of his last 10 seasons.

Mike, despite all the hype, can't seem to hit the ball over the fence for the first 10 years of his career. He then decides to hit the weight room after that 10th season then explodes for 50 home runs in each of his last 10 seasons. When they both retire at age 40, Bryce finishes with 600 home runs and Mike with 500.

Even though Mike Trout hit 50 home runs in 10 seasons and the most Bryce hit in a season was 40, because Bryce started earlier and was consistent he finished with more home runs. Mike had to work much harder in the second half of his career to catch up.

Now you will notice this was an extremely simple example that did not include compounding. If we introduced compounding, where the home runs get compounded on with interest, Bryce Harper would be way ahead of Mike Trout because he started earlier and allowed his home runs to compound on each other.

It's not impossible for Mike to catch up, just very challenging. And if Bryce had hit 50 home runs instead of 40? Mike wouldn't even be a comparison. Not a hall of fame player anymore.

Recently, there have been people pushing for the idea that you should wait to save when you're in your middle years where you have a higher income and your costs become more normal after paying down student loans and other debt. That is craziness.

We just looked at the power of compounding and how time makes investing much simpler. If you wait to save when you have more income you lose the power of compounding the longer you wait. And truth is, even if you make more money, our human nature is to spend it.

Building wealth has little to do with your income or investment returns and lots to do with your savings rate. You don't need more income, you need more saving. You can build wealth without a high income but have no chance without a high savings rate, so it's clear which one matters more.

Past a certain level of income, what you need is just what sits below your ego. Everyone needs the basics, and once the basics are covered there's another level of comfortable basics, that adds entertainment, and enlightening. But spending with a high sense of materialism is a way to spend money to show people that you have (or had) money. One of the most powerful ways to increase your savings isn't to raise your income, but your humility.

At the end of the day, procrastination is your enemy. If you have put off saving for retirement up until now, start saving right now and start saving a lot. Like my simple math showed in the previous chapter with Auston Matthews and Patrik Laine, the longer you delay, the more delayed your retirement date becomes or the more you will have to save to catch up. There is nothing fancy or complicated other than disciplined saving.

Don't panic and follow the advice from an old Chinese proverb.

"The best time to plant a tree was 20 years ago. The second best time is now."

Or the advice from Nike.

THE GAME PLAN

"Just Do It"

Or me.

"Just Start Saving".

10. RISK MANAGEMENT
(CONTROL WHAT YOU CAN CONTROL)

"I have a plan of action, but the game is a game of adjustments."
- Mike Krzyzewski

THE GAME PLAN

In the world of finance, risk is a word you hear on a daily basis. Risk measurement, risk parity, risk controls, risk tolerance, risk-adjusted returns. Risk management is big business on Wall Street/Bay Street/Money Street/Any Street.

Basically, if you are investing, there will always be something to worry about because you are putting your money to work in today's complex markets, which are full of uncertainty. It doesn't matter if you work for Goldman Sachs or if you're an individual saving for a house or retirement, we all have to deal with the fact that none of us know how the future will play out, especially in the financial markets.

A general theory when looking at investment risk is the younger you are, the more ability you have to take on risk because you have a longer time horizon - 20 or 30 years, for example - with many years to invest until retirement and start drawing upon it. Also, you can make the assumption that your salary will increase in the future, so you will have the ability to replenish losses over time with your increased savings.

In sports, your peak physical years are between the years of 20-30. Most athletes can afford to take risk because they have the athletic ability to either recover or have a game based more on speed. Past 30 (aside from a few players such as LeBron James and Hayley Wickenheiser...) many athletes bodies are either worn down from the physicality and just naturally slow down a touch which means their games have to change in order to continue to compete. They can't take some of the risks they once did because their time horizon has shrunk.

So if you are a younger investor with a long time horizon you are likely to make more money holding a sizable portion of your portfolio in stocks or other assets with a high-expected rate of return. That's because historically, stocks offer greater returns than "safer" alternatives such as Government Treasury bonds over the long term.

But in the short term, stocks tend to be much more volatile. So as people age and get closer to retirement, it is recommended that you shift more assets to the "safer than stocks" category such as government bonds, corporate bonds and even GIC's.

In retirement you will need your investments to fund your everyday spending needs so your ability to take risk has shrunk considerably because there is much less time to make up for any losses in stocks. If the stock market suddenly crashes and your savings go down 20 or 30 percent, you will then be forced to sell your stocks at a low price. However, if you're younger and stocks crash, you can just hang tight and wait for the market to recover.

But it's not all about age; it's also about your willingness to take on risk. You may be young and have the ability to take on fairly aggressive investment risk, but this may be out of your comfort zone. In this case you may take on less risky investments to help you sleep at night. Not everyone can stomach a decline of 20% in their portfolio so combining stocks with bonds makes sense.

Investing isn't just about maximizing returns. It's about getting the returns you need to achieve your goals and doesn't cause more stress than it needs to be. So even though bonds are very likely to have lower returns in the future than they did historically, it doesn't mean investors shouldn't include them in their portfolios.

You need to make sure that you remain with a good balance between being safe with your investments and taking risk in the markets. You may think that cash or bonds aren't risky in the sense that they don't fluctuate as much as stocks, but you need to take inflation into account. Inflation takes away purchasing power, which could be detrimental when it comes to meeting your long-term needs.

No One size fits all

When it comes to investing there is no such thing as one size fits all. No two investors are the same, just like in a sports team; no two players are the same (unless you're the Vancouver Canucks Sedin twins - that is the only exception). Different players will respond to different situations differently, such as certain coaching styles or some players prefer to pass rather than shoot. You need to know what you are most comfortable with and build your investment portfolios and financial plan around that.

If you can't shoot a basketball and someone tells you to start shooting 3 pointers to get more points - that may work for them if they are good and comfortable with shooting 3 pointers, but you may not be comfortable with risking those deep shots when you would prefer to go for the easy layup.

Or in a hockey game and you are down by a couple goals, you may need to change tactics and take on some more risk to get those extra goals such as hanging by the opposing team blue line for a breakaway pass, taking extra bumps in front of the net to get a goal or even pull your goalie for an extra attacker. These situations can help produce more goals but also can put the team at risk because they are out of defensive positions or leave their net exposed.

Same thing goes in investing. Risk is related to reward. The higher the risk you take, such as putting more money to stocks, you are hoping to get rewarded for this act with higher returns.

You may not be comfortable with putting all your money in stocks because it is too risky for you. However, diversification and mixing in some 3-point shots with layups and dunks (or stocks and bonds) will help your portfolio achieve solid returns for your risk level and achieve your goals.

You see, even though someone may not be comfortable with shooting 3 pointers (let's say putting money into stocks) you still need to make some 3 pointers to win the game because against another team that shoots 3 pointers a lot (Michigan State's Tori Jankoska or Steph Curry and the Golden State Warriors) you will lose and not achieve your goals.

Like I explained before, there is no one-size-fits-all when it comes to risk tolerance, it is specific to each individual. Risk-averse investors may want to hold a combination of a conservative model portfolio and cash, which will reduce overall risk. As wealth increases, tolerance for risk may increase. As investors grow older, tolerance for risk may decrease. It is important that you constantly update your risk profile and make sure your portfolio matches their risk preferences and current life stage situation.

11. ESTATE PLANNING: INSURANCE/WILL (WHAT HAPPENS NEXT)

"In this world nothing can be said to be certain, except death and taxes"
- Benjamin Franklin

In school, when kids are asked what they want to be when they grow up many will say pop star, tech entrepreneur or professional athlete. Why not pro athlete? Those that make it can get paid a lot of money to play sports, get sponsorships and compete with the best. Despite the glamour and seeing an athlete-business whiz like LeBron James or Magic Johnson, there are many more who squander their earnings by getting involved in sketchy investments and living beyond their means.

I mentioned earlier in the book how many athletes are in financial trouble only a few years removed from retiring from their sports. And the length of a career even if you do make it isn't as long as it seems. The graph below from The Wall Street Journal shows the average length of an NFL career continues to decrease.

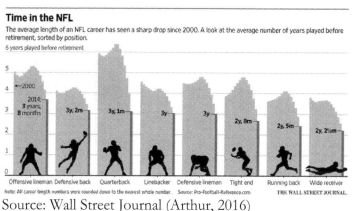

Source: Wall Street Journal (Arthur, 2016)

This means that it is important that athletes develop more financial knowledge and prepare for their future after sport just like everyone should be doing.

This can be a very overwhelming prospect, especially since many athletes will have little experience outside the sporting realm and many may have missed out on college or university educations due to their sporting commitments.

More and more athletes are now taking steps to plan for life after sport well before their retirement from competition to make the transition easier.

At Harvard Business School, professor Anita Elberse, wanted to change the trend of athletes squandering their earnings very quickly after their careers and help them make more of a difference. In Fall 2017, they launched a semester-long program called "Crossover into Business" which gives active and recently active professional athletes the chance to develop their business acumen and explore business interests with the help of MBA student-mentors (Rollins, 2019). The athletes remotely work throughout the semester on a set of cases and other topics of interest and deliver a final presentation at the end of the semester. Current and former stars such as Kyrie Irving, Chris Bosh and players from other professional sports including the WNBA, NFL, NHL, MLS and UFC have taken her course (Rollins, 2019).

Jamal Murray, one of the rising stars in the NBA and used his platform and wealth to benefit a community centre in Kitchener, Ontario. The centre provides a safe place for at-risk-kids to come and develop a love for sports. It allows kids to build relationships, find mentors and reach their goals. Jamal Murray played at this community centre growing up. He used his platform to be bigger than basketball and leave a legacy beyond the court planning for when his career and life comes to an end. It is amazing to see the difference it can make when someone takes the time to plan for things bigger than themselves that will last beyond their lifetimes.

Just like how athletes' professional careers will come to an end, life here on earth is not permanent and we need to be prepared for when that time comes. Now I know this isn't the most exciting or uplifting topic but is one of the most important aspects in planning. Things such as having an estate plan, wills and life insurance can bring peace of mind and security for families and make sure generations that follow are taken care of.

The Not so Boring intro to Life Insurance

I don't think anyone really likes to talk about life insurance. Probably because life insurance is a very adulty thing to do (and many of us don't want to grow up), it's boring, it's moderately expensive and also the fact that it is a very morbid concept. After spending a couple years auditing insurance clients, I can confirm that it is a very boring but important business.

So, you may ask, why do it? Wouldn't that money be better off investing in the market or spent on that trip to Hawaii because we're all supposed to be living in the moment anyway?

Well, the short answer is: You get insurance because, after you die all of a sudden with nothing to pass down to help your loved ones, you don't really want the people you love living in a cardboard box, mad that you never took care of their futures. It makes financial sense.

If you want to know if you really need life insurance, take a look at your personal situation. Basically, if you have children, or a spouse, or anyone else who depends on you financially, then life insurance is probably for you.

Especially if you have debts, mortgages, loans, and other things that those nice people are going to be liable for paying if you pass away. If your bank accounts don't have enough money in it to cover the living expenses of those nice people who depend on you then you definitely should have life insurance.

If you don't have any dependents, then there's no real need for insurance (as your estate should be able to pay for your internment). In other words, single people and children have no need for insurance because they have no dependents, but married people and (especially) parents need plenty.

If you have your family depending on you financially and you don't have insurance in place to cover for them if you pass away, it can be much like if your baseball team only has one pitcher.

Let's say that one pitcher is an absolute star. I'm talking 8-time Cy Young winner, rarely loses games, pitches a complete game every game and averages 10 strikeouts a game. Because that pitcher is so good, the team never considered getting another one if this one will give them the best chance to win every game and win the championship every year.

Then that pitcher goes down with a career ending injury half way through the season. Since the team never got additional pitchers, players from the team are forced to try and pitch to keep the team afloat. While they try their best, the team doesn't win at the same pace and are now playing behind a lot.

This can be the situation if you don't utilize life insurance to protect your family, especially in those key earnings years between ages 25-45 where you most likely have a spouse and kids who depend on the income brought in to provide for the family.

Your biggest asset is not your house, car or investments. Your biggest asset is YOU and your ability to earn income. If you pass away, money that your family assumed will always be coming in, isn't coming in anymore to pay for future expenses that continue after you're gone (i.e. university tuition, mortgage).

So, if you have people that depend on you, then it is important that you have something in place like life insurance to ensure your family continues to live life as normal as possible. Unexpected death would be sad for your loved ones, don't make it sad *and* expensive.

The Golden State Warriors are arguably the best team in NBA history (here come the hot takes). They are loaded with star players like Steph Curry, Klay Thompson and Draymond Green. If one of those players went down, the team would be in trouble so what they did is they went and added insurance by getting Kevin Durant (arguably the best scorer in basketball) and other players like Andre

Iguodala, Sean Livingston that would provide protection if a star player went down.

You are your families star player. Make sure you add insurance like Kevin Durant to protect your family's future.

Options, Options, Options...

There are plenty of options when it comes to life insurance but the common-sense advice is to keep it simple and cost effective. For most people, the answer is something called "term life" insurance. This type of policy means you pay a premium every year for a certain number of years, typically 10, 20 or 30 years. It's the same amount every year, determined when you get the policy.

Term life insurance is basic, easy to understand and generally inexpensive. You buy a term life insurance policy for a specific period of time (hence the phrase "term") generally 10, 20, 30 years. The amount of coverage is generally in the $250,000 to $1 million range, which depends on your personal situation with factors such as income, assets, and liabilities.

If you die during that period of time, the insurer pays the coverage amount of money to the beneficiary (the person you told them to pay when you got the policy). If you don't die (good for you), the policy expires worthless and you never see that money again. It's as simple as that. This would be the equivalent of paying for car insurance and never getting in an accident. It's nice to know its there if you really need it but hope it never comes to that.

Some good news is that the cost of term life insurance is pretty reasonable especially if you are in your 20's, 30's and even 40's. In your 20's and 30s, average monthly premiums range from $10-28 a month, which is not even a night out to dinner. For those in their 40s and more likely to have children you can have peace of mind for less than $100 a month. That's a pretty good deal.

Another good thing is that life insurance proceeds are not taxable when they payout to beneficiaries. One less thing to worry about if something unexpected happens.

There are other options to term insurance, which tend to be more complicated and for different circumstance such as whole-life, universal, variable life, variable universal, etc. This sounds interesting but in the end you pay more expensive premiums and can get more than you bargained for. These options really only make sense for the wealthy who have complicated tax structures and estates to worry about. For the general person, it is best to keep it simple and stick with term life insurance.

Will's for the Win

It doesn't matter if you're three time London and New York marathon winner, Paula Radcliffe. It also doesn't matter if Shaquille O'Neal is your palm reader and told you you'll live a really long time. It doesn't even matter how old you are unless you're, like, 13 (and if you are 13, well I applaud you for reading a financial book, young middle schooler! Your Future You thanks you!). When talking about a will, it is important that old people have one, but a will isn't just for old people.

OKAY, I know what you're thinking: Here I am trying to play Chel 19 (NHL 19 video game for those who need translating), and you're making me think, about my mortality—it's kind of ruining my day. But think of it as a way to be a thoughtful (and responsible) person. Because that's what a will really is: a will is a way to maintain peaceful relationships among loved ones. It's a legal document that imposes your final wishes that they have to listen to and respect. Having an action plan and instructions so that when you pass away everything is transitioned seamlessly.

Much like in sports, people know that even your best player can't play forever. The teams that can continue to stay on top have plans in place to transition smoothly once their best players retire. The Detroit Red Wings and San Antonio Spurs are two franchises that have been on top for many years that prepared certain players and systems so that when their best players like Steve Yzerman, Nicklas Lidstrom or Tim Duncan, David Robinson retired they have players groomed to fill those roles like Pavel Datsyuk, Henrik Zetterberg and Kawhi Leonard, LaMarcus Aldridge.

Kentucky Wildcats in college basketball know that every year their roster will be turned over by players heading to the NBA. In preparation they already have their recruits chosen for next year so that their team continues their success.

You should start to think about a will once you move out of the house and enter the workforce. Why? Because you are probably now accumulating stuff such as bank accounts, investment portfolios and even your car and other personal items.

By the time you are married and into parenthood, then that is when most experts say that having a will should move from a should to a must. If you have a child, you need a will. Even if you're a 28-year-old Olympian in perfect health. For a parent, the most important decision will be whom he or she wants to take care of the kids. That is something you are for sure going to want to say in a will!

If your children are under the age of 18, you'll have to appoint guardians to take care of them. So, consider these things: Where do you want your children to be raised? Who do you trust most as a parental figure? Who is going to work best with your executor (the person you assign to carry out your wills instructions)? Your executor and guardian can be the same person as well.

Okay, I know this chapter hasn't been a very uplifting subject, but I hope that I at least made it topics to consider and maybe change the negative light held on these things such as life insurance and wills.

The key point I wanted to finish with is this, obviously we all would hope we would never need to use these insurance policies or have to think about wills for when we pass away, but you will sleep better at night knowing that those nice people that you love called your family, will be taken care of if something should ever happen to you.

12. GENERAL MANAGER
(IT'S OKAY TO ASK FOR HELP)

"The investor's chief problem – and even his worst enemy – is likely to be himself."
- Benjamin Graham

THE GAME PLAN

In professional sports, most teams have a general manager to help them with player personnel decisions. These general managers have an overview of the entire team and generally have experience in the different aspects of the organizations to help make decisions that are best for the team as a whole. The players are focused on their individual tasks and by having the general manager and coaching staff provide structure and a plan is key to successful teams.

The Dallas Cowboys have done things a little different than most NFL and professional sports teams where their owner Jerry Jones has the unique role of being both owner and general manager of the team. In fact, Jerry Jones hasn't hired a general manager since he became owner of the team in 1989.

For the Cowboys, the general manager position is unique in that Jerry has the ultimate power in being the owner, but he also has all the rest of the Dallas Cowboys franchise to handle, including the ownership responsibilities he has to fulfil for the NFL, the highly profitable operation of AT&T Stadium, and the marketing arm of the organization.

Because he manages so many different areas and doesn't specialize specifically on the team, Jerry has been known to make football related decisions based mostly on impulse and guesswork and the Cowboys franchise has largely been disorganized.

This has led to some very poor team results and decisions that have caused fans and players to leave scratching their heads.

Recently, Jerry Jones is exhibiting a degree of trust in his two main football advisors, which has led too much better football team decisions and results. The biggest reason he now relies on these two men is because he has long histories where they know him well and how to work with him. It is built on trust.

And for the first time under Jerry, the team was going for decidedly unflashy but ultimately very productive draft picks such as strong offensive linemen.

He still is deeply involved in decisions about the acquisition and retention of players. He is just far more likely to take the other's viewpoint over his own, once again because of that trust factor.

In similar ways, people often don't reach out for help with their finances, whether it's from a financial planner, estate planner, accountant or someone they trust. There can be many reasons why:

- People are overconfident
- They think that they will eventually make a lot of money with their own decisions
- They think they can form a foolproof investing strategy by reading the news
- They think they are investing but really, they are speculating
- They think they can handle how their estate will be administered

Another reason people tend to avoid reaching out for help is that they feel guilty or ashamed about their financial shortcomings or the mistakes they've made. This is probably the biggest barrier for people asking for help, yet it is so important that they do so they can get back on the right track.

There are many great new platforms coming out such as "robo-advisors" that simplify the investment process, which is great for investors all around. When they first came out, they threatened to replace human advisors in situations where not much human help was needed such as investing in model portfolios for smaller accounts. These services are very good for young, tech savvy individuals with their efficient digital on boarding and getting started in investing.

Increasingly, these robo-advisor platforms are teaming up with human advisors in new and creative ways to provide "hybrid" combinations that achieve the best of both worlds. These platforms can take care of smart and cost-effective investing while still providing the human element and value of advice when it comes to people with their finances.

Of course, you could Google and read a bunch of blogs but having someone who knows you personally and your situation sets yourself up for greater success.

If you need a comprehensive financial plan or want help coping with a market meltdown, you're likely to want to turn to a trusted human advisor with high levels of financial expertise but also human qualities like communication skills and empathy because emotions are the greatest factor for success in investing and financial planning.

The Intelligence Curse - it's okay to ask for help

Some of the smartest people outside the world of finance can also be terrible investors. Doctors, lawyers, and engineers are some of the most intelligent, most educated people around. They have all put in years of study and advanced training into their professions. They know a lot of things in their fields of study yet many in this group (not all, of course) tend to be poor investors.

Why?

Because most assume success or wealth in one arena (their career) will easily translate into another (investing in the markets). Smart people are often the most dangerous in terms of poor investment decision-making ability because they tend to be overconfident, make things too complex, and over-think things.

As I've touched on before, the biggest risk we all take is letting our emotions drive our decisions. Fear and greed can lead to anxiety that causes us to make choices we will regret. For many of us it probably makes good sense to get some outside expert advice to help manage these emotions. For intelligent people, it's okay to say "I don't know" from time to time.

Mark Scheifele, one of the best players in the NHL who obviously knows how to play hockey at a high level, still hires skills coaches like Hall of Famer Adam Oates, trainers to help build a strong frame and nutritionists to help ensure he is healthy, motivated, hold him accountable and push him to be better.

When it comes to choosing someone like a financial planner to help you with your finances, take your time and talk to multiple advisors and connections before making a decision. Have tons of questions prepared such as experience/education, processes, fee structure, philosophies and references. Make sure that you are confident that they will have your best interests in mind and that you are comfortable with them not only as an investor and planner but as a person. As in any relationship, trust is key.

Learning from mistakes

People need to realize that they can learn from mistakes, so they can improve. Everyone makes mistakes whether it be investing, playing sports or trying to build that IKEA bookshelf. They key is how you respond to them.

In golf, most golfers overestimate their abilities when they use specialized clubs designed to optimize distance and control. According to lots of research, poor club selection was the main reason why approach shots landed short of the green (Giordano, 2018). Why? Golfers choose their club based on how far the ball would travel if they hit their best shot.

For example, say you are 180 yards away from the hole that carries over a pond. You have made that distance with your 4 irons before if you hit it like you can but might be better to layup with an 8 iron and keep the ball in play. You decide to go with the 4 iron, chunk up a bunch of grass when you hit the ball which then flies right into the water which then results in you tossing your clubs in the water with it.

Before you stomp off the course (and have to buy new clubs), acknowledge the mistake, figure out what you did wrong and how you can do better next time. Did you need to have a different club to make it over or is it really out of range and you should layup for a better shot next? Learning from mistakes in any aspect of life is how you get better.

13. COMPETITION
(STRONGER AND FASTER AND LUCKIER)

"You've got to look for tough competition you've got to want to beat the best"
-Grete Waitz

It would be impossible to look at today's professional athletes as a whole and argue that they are not better than the athletes in the past. They continue to become faster and stronger, not to mention more skilled, better coached, better equipped, better nourished and better prepared more than ever. Sports have continued to evolve from a time where players and teams were less complex and more like the average man.

In today's sports, we have incredible cyborgs such as Serena Williams, who can serve a tennis ball in excess of 115 miles per hour and is the most dominant force in tennis - men's or women's. We have freak athletes such as LeBron James, who can log enormous minutes playing in every situation and never seem to get tired. We have kids such as Auston Matthews and Saquan Barkley, who could have walked into an NHL and NFL dressing rooms as rookies and not looked out of place from a body-type standpoint.

When professional hockey began in the NHL, it drew only white players from Canada, mainly Ontario and Quebec. But over time, the league began recruiting players from all over Canada and then the U.S and eventually from all races and from all around the world. This greatly expanded the pool of talent. Players from Russia, Sweden, Finland, Czech Republic and Slovakia brought a new level of skill to the game. Diversity has allowed sports to have an even higher standard of success.

In addition, training has improved greatly since the early beginnings. 20-25 years ago, players would finish their hockey season and go home for the summer to play different sports like baseball and a couple weeks before the season start to lift weights and get into shape. Now every player in the league is year-round training trying to get an edge into next season.

In today's game, players are better than ever which are largely the reason games are lower scoring. Many will argue the small gap between the best and worst players in the NHL is so small now it's created a game in which it's more difficult to create offense. And I've barely mentioned the advancements in goaltending and their techniques and coaching which has also contributed to making it more difficult to score goals.

Stronger, faster, and luckier

Stephen Jay Gould was a renowned biologist at Harvard University who loved to write about baseball. He once did an in-depth study to figure out why no player in Major League Baseball had maintained a batting average of more than .400 for a full season since Ted Williams hit .406 in 1941 (Gould, 2004).

The players were leap years better than when Ted Williams played so there had to be an explanation as to why nobody could cross that .400 average. Gould considered several conventional explanations, including more night games, demanding travel, improved fielding, and more extensive use of relief pitching. None of these provided an explanation.

He came to the conclusion that as skill improves for the population, luck becomes more important in determining results. On average, players have greater skill today than they did in years past, but their outcomes are more tied to luck (Gould, 2004).

Many things have to go right for players to stay at the top of their game. A couple missed chances; one more goal or a couple key injuries can affect performance that you have no control over or predicting. This extends to other realms as well such as investing.

Same with sports, lots of things have to go right in order for an outperforming manager to stay on top. Vanguard, the second largest asset manager in the world, looked at the performance after a fund received a Morningstar rating.

The Morningstar ratings are based on a funds record over the previous 3, 5 and 10-year periods. There is a heavy bias towards the recent short-term results but over the long term the "reversion to the mean" comes into effect. According to a 2014 study by the Wall Street Journal (Constable & Espinoza, 2014), only 14% of five-star funds in 2004 still held that rating a decade later and approximately 50% dropped to three or fewer stars.

We can't all be above average investors because the market, like sports (unless it's ties in soccer) is a zero-sum game. There will be winners and there will be losers and they'll cancel each other out.

The reversion to the mean concept poses a powerful force on mutual fund returns. Just like we assume that Connor McDavid will be the best player for the next 30 years, many people assume that manager skill will persist, but it doesn't. Connor McDavid will eventually age, lose his speed and revert to more of an average player and by then he will most likely retire. And managers whose records substantially exceed industry norms will return to the average or below.

Hedge fund manager John Paulson managed a fund that compounded at 13.9% annually over twenty years when the S&P 500 did 9.2% over the same period (Stevenson & Goldstein, 2017). His results became famous and people poured money into the fund assuming this must go on forever. However, his fund that destroyed for two decades got destroyed shortly thereafter. Over the next four years, his fund would lose 43% of its value. Well, surely stocks must have had a rough time too right? Wrong. The S&P 500 **grew** 57% over the same time. And in the nine years since the great recession in 2009, Paulson is down 21%. The S&P 500 is up 259%.

Now I'm not saying this always happens, in fact, it is great that you are investing in the first place and many of these funds help people achieve their goals which is the main goal of investing. I'm just saying it is extremely tough to pick the winners, even if their past returns have been excellent. You might outperform, or you might underperform. And to outperform the market's return, you have to outperform the majority of others who are also trying to outperform the market's return.

At the end of the day you have the option to 1) try and beat the market or 2) match the market's returns through an index fund or ETF. And you have to consider costs with both options.

Money managers don't work for free (who does?) and they have to charge investors enough to cover expenses and make a profit. The managers are already faced with the difficult task of beating the market, but they also have to do this by a wide enough margin to subtract the costs over around 2-2.5% a year and still beat an index fund.

Truth is that investors who buy market-matching index funds and ETFs will outperform the majority of investors who attempt to outperform market-matching index funds. So actually, just matching the market automatically makes you an above average investor (might need to re-read and think on that for a second).

Competition in investing has increased over the years with factors such as faster access to information and increase in number of mutual funds which has tripled in the past 20 years.

Active managers have had a tough time beating the index not because they lack skill, but because they're opponents have increased in number and in talent. The challenge of increased competition is because most investment firms have access to the same information, supercomputer software, and sharp MBA/PhD/CFA/CPA students.

Because of reversion to the mean, outperformers are far more likely to come back down to the average than they are to continue their ascent. Investors, like professional athletes have gotten bigger, stronger and faster, which is why luck will continue to be a much bigger determiner of success than it was in the past.

THE GAME PLAN

In sports, the more you train, practice, and try switching things up in your game you are generally rewarded with positive results.

But in investing, it doesn't work that way. More resources, more time spent, more effort, etc. does not necessarily lead to better outcomes. We are provided with proof every year as smart, well-connected investors go through rises, falls and sometimes disasters turning over their funds to chase performance benchmarks.

I know, I know, it doesn't seem that exciting to say that working harder doesn't usually produce the end results you're trying to generate. But if anything, trying harder can result in over trading or many other behaviours that can end up eating into potential returns.

If returns were based simply by trying harder than the people who trade all day, every day would be the wealthiest. In reality and from findings, it works in the opposite way.

Now I'm not forcing you to choose index funds over mutual funds. If the opportunity to try and beat the market excites you then go for it (don't try and do it with all your money) I'm just laying out the concepts for you to decide.

Long-term, common sense investing points towards index funds and I'm not the only one that says that - even some of the top money managers admit that index funds are the best option for investors.

Jack R. Meyer, former president of the Harvard Endowment who tripled the fund from $8 billion to $27 billion, had this to say what investors should do with their money: "avoid the most hyped and expensive funds, in favour of low-cost index funds and invest for the long-term.

Warren Buffett in his 2013 shareholder letter described the instructions in his will for managing his wife's trust. He directed the trustees to invest 90% of the assets in a "very low-cost S&P 500 index fund.

Then listen to William F. Sharpe, professor of finance at Stanford University and Nobel Prize winner who said, "The simplest way of investing in the market is via a very broadly diversified, very low-cost index fund. You can do it in other ways that would be a lot more expensive. But at least worry a lot about diversification and cost."

14. PATIENCE
(WHY LEAF FANS WOULD MAKE GREAT INVESTORS)

"The most important attribute for success in investing is patience, patience and more patience. The majority of investors do not possess this characteristic."
-Peter Cundill

THE GAME PLAN

It's a little-known secret that the Toronto Maple Leafs have gone a long, long, longgggggg time without winning the Stanley Cup. The last time the Toronto Maple Leafs won the Stanley Cup was in 1967. To put it in perspective how long ago that was, this is what the world looked like in 1967:

- Canadians who were in their mid-teens then are either retired now or looking forward to retirement.
- The first McDonald's restaurant in Canada opened in B.C. in 1967
- Man still had not landed on the moon (happened 2 years later in July 1969)
- The first countertop microwave was introduced in 1967; which is now a staple in how I make popcorn.
- Typewriters gave way to computers and the Internet.
- A Toronto detached home that sold for $20,000, could now fetch $1 million plus.
- The price of a litre of gasoline was 7.2 cents/litre
- The CN Tower wasn't built yet.
- Maple Leaf Gardens still stands but is now a Loblaw's grocery store and athletic centre for Ryerson University. Air Canada Centre is now the home for the Leafs and the Toronto Raptors NBA franchise.

Yes, it has been a long time. The Toronto Maple Leafs have the longest Cup drought in the NHL as it's been over 50 years since they last won the most coveted prize in hockey.

For many of these years, the Leafs were characterized by short term decision making which led them nowhere in the standings, teams experienced constant roster overhaul, and they were known for buying players based on previous success but paid high prices for them.

They now have a blueprint in place building slowly with an eye on the future. They have got their fans to focus on long-term thinking and success has come along with that. Same thing with investing and thinking long term, short-term thinking is dangerous. Reading the day-to-day news is probably the worst thing you can do as an investor because it causes fast, irrational decisions.

Patience and Trust in the Plan Throughout the Chaos

Give leaf fans credit with their patience throughout all these years. They have learned from their previous mistakes which is the best thing you can do in anything. When you're living in or looking on at the day-to-day chaos of Leaf land, all you see are small, constant and usually inconsequential crises. It creates the disastrous habit of thinking the next game or the next month is all that matters or that if a player is in a slump we need to get rid of him. That tendency has repeatedly infected previous regimes, drawing them into terrible, short-term decision-making, and not helping the long-term future of the team.

Despite all the chaos, most Leaf fans remain loyal. Throughout the ups and downs and being at the bad end of most jokes, the fans have continued to support the team. They have had many bad directions in the past but have now come to realize that creating a plan and sticking to it is the best formula for long-term success. And the best minds in the business and investing world understand the same thing.

Amazon founder and CEO Jeff Bezos was once asked "Jeff, what's the best advice Warren Buffett ever gave to you?"

Bezos: "I asked Warren, your investment thesis is so simple...you're the second richest guy in the world, and it's so simple. Why doesn't everyone just copy you?"

Buffett: "Because nobody wants to get rich slow."

Bringing in great leadership such as Brendan Shanahan, Lou Lamoriello to go along with bright young minds in young GM Kyle Dubas has created an ecosystem designed for stability and success. This means a new philosophy of starting from the ground up and on building slowly through the draft and long-term projects, rather than quick fixes via trades for established players.

Starting over is no guarantee for success. The Edmonton Oilers haven't seemed to figure it out despite landing Connor McDavid and the Chicago Blackhawks suffered for a while until they made it work. However, everyone at every level has accepted that the other way – the way the Leafs had been trying for about a decade – only brings mediocrity and disappointment. The hard part is staying with the hard road down, which eventually leads back up.

The Leafs management realised what works for good investors also works for professional sports. Taking the slow, yet calculated approach to building a team and investment portfolio brings high probability of success compared to those that aim for the quick fix.

Learning from Mistakes

Much good can come from the bad times in our lives, whether it be new opportunities or merely personal growth. From talking to various mentors and from personal experience, the mistakes and rough patches in life provide the greatest lessons and guidance for future success. While it is tough to swallow, it brings knowledge and perseverance.

No investor is perfect. Every investor, including Warren Buffett, has made mistakes and lost some money along the way. It is not easy riding the ups and downs of the market but that's how investors improve. The hardest thing to do in investing is when market crashes or downturns come, is not abandoning the plan. When disaster strikes, and the markets go down, the biggest thing is to stick to the process because the road back up is great. This would be the worst time to jump ship.

In sports, no season will ever be absolutely perfect. There are losses, injuries, friction with team chemistry and bad plays will be made. But the successful teams take all these variables and drive themselves towards success.

Warren Buffett's biggest key to his success is not by picking the best stocks but that he never wavered from his plan. Even when his portfolio was getting hammered by over 50%, he never sold once, and he rose up through those patches better than anyone. That takes incredible will and trust in the plan to not sell when you've lost half your money.

When looking at market returns over a long period of time, it looks like a long, smooth, steady ascent. The chart below takes a look at the Dow Jones returns over a 32-year period. Over this time a gain of 1786% was realized.

Source: Yahoo Finance

However, in the short-term, it looks a lot more like the Swiss Alps – with peaks and descents all over the map. The chart below shows the Toronto Stock Exchange (TSX) from January 2018 to September 2018.

THE GAME PLAN

Source: Bloomberg

My advice to investors is to expect rough patches in the market, don't be surprised when they come. And stick to your game plan. Roadblocks will come your way but don't let that get in the way of success.

Since no one knows when the roadblocks or high-rises will come, the best thing for investors to do when looking long-term is invest a portion of your income each month. That way, the risk of buying everything at its peak can be minimized. This is known as dollar-cost-averaging and can be set up automatically with your financial institutions to make it seamless.

15. WHEN THE GAME PLAN CHANGES

"I can't change the direction of the wind, but I can adjust my sails to always reach my destination."
- Jimmy Dean

THE GAME PLAN

If there is one thing that we can all be certain of in life, it is having to adapt to change. Things are always changing right around us from the weather, to the news, to your clothes (unless you wear the same thing every day). In sports it is no different and many times, change can happen unexpectedly.

There can be injuries throughout the season, players demanding trades, trades out of the blue and underperformance. Players and teams have to learn how to deal with these potential scenarios to continue down the paths to success.

Recently, there seems to be a lot more players demanding trades from teams, specifically in the NBA. Players seem to want to link up with certain players or go to destinations where they can fulfil their potential.

Kyrie Irving did this in the 2017 offseason with the Cleveland Cavaliers. He had good runs to the finals, including a championship, alongside LeBron James when he suddenly wanted to leave and play elsewhere. This caught the Cavaliers off guard but they granted his wish and shipped him off to Boston.

The Cavaliers had to change their future plans, which had included Kyrie as their main point guard scorer, and adjust their team structure to remain successful. They retooled with different types of players and were able to continue on to the finals again without Kyrie.

A team coming in with high expectations but underperforming has also got to be one of the most frustrating things in sports, for the players, coaches and fans. The 2017-2018 Edmonton Oilers had one of those seasons where dreams of lifting the cup were quickly shattered as the team never really got it together.

Coming in with reigning NHL scoring champ, Connor McDavid, and other offensive weapons like Leon Draisaitl, expectations were sky-high. However, defensive struggles and lack of secondary scoring to help McDavid piled up too many loses and failed to even make playoffs.

The team had to change their approach and realized they needed to retool in certain areas in order to improve and get to championship level hockey.

Change can be good as you can learn more about yourself, find ways to improve and get better each and every day. Even changes that can be seen as disappointing can help you get better and learn how to adjust to change. Over the course of life, you'll go through many changes that will likely affect your personal finances.

The past few years have made me realize that my financial plan, investment plan or job title will never matter as much as having a safe, secure and healthy family. Everything else is cherry on top.

Don't get me wrong - saving, investing, financial planning, keeping money and job stress low are still priorities. It's just that some priorities will have to take back seat to new priorities such as spending time with family, friends and people you love. Making sure you are ready for whatever life may bring you.

Financial Planning is a Process, Not an Event

THE GAME PLAN

Creating a financial plan is not a one-time deal. It's an ongoing process that is always evolving as life throws curve balls time and time again.

Just like general managers don't just assemble their team then sit on their hands for 20 years, you cannot sit on your hands and not adjust and tweak your plan as life comes.

What happens when you decide to get married, buy a house, receive an inheritance, get into a health crisis (COVID-19) or even retirement? These things can be much better managed when you are prepared with a plan and constantly evolving your plan to help you achieve your desired goals.

Before any sports season begins, teams set out goals that they want to achieve in order to provide direction for all the moving parts to come together. It could include reaching a certain number of wins, personal milestones and of course winning the championship at the end. Throughout the season, even as different changes and unforeseen events happen, the team adjusts its systems to continue on towards the goal. If they didn't, the whole team would fall astray.

The financial planning process is no different, where it starts out with carefully thought-out goals and providing the tools and resources around it to carry out these goals. Without going through this process, you would be wasting valuable resources on purposes that may ultimately not be in your best interest.

THE GAME PLAN

Planning out your finances once is the easy part. Planning over and over again is not, yet it is important for navigating the hard-hitting gridiron of life.

16. KNOW THE RULES TO WIN THE GAME

"A young man knows the rules, but the old man knows the exceptions."
-Oliver Wendell Holmes, Sr.

Knowing the rules of the game and using them to your advantage is what separates good coaches from average coaches. Love him or hate him, Bill Belichick is arguably the best coach in sports at knowing the rulebook and using it to his advantage. And because he knows the rules, he knows how to use them to win the game.

Belichick doesn't just know the rules, he obsesses over them unlike any other coach and his players know what they can and can't do. The Patriots understand the rules and even individual referee's tendencies. The Patriots knowledge of the rulebook is not just to keep players from getting penalties but also to keep them disciplined in their techniques and give them a game-planning edge.

An example of Belichick's mastery is in the 2016 season. That year, the NFL introduced a new rule to make the kick-offs safer. They decided to bring out kickoff touchbacks to the 25-yard line, figuring that kick-off returners would have more incentive to down the ball in the end zone now that they were getting 5 free yards for doing so. Seemed like a logical idea on the surface. But the NFL didn't see the game the way Bill Belichick sees the game.

Given the speed of the kick, return team and cover team, most initial collisions on the kick-off happen around the 15-yard line, meaning the returner has about 10 more yards to get to the 25 (Chase, 2016). It may not sound like it but getting to the 25 is much harder than it seems. What Belichick decided to do instead of giving the other team the 25 was make sure the kick-off lands inside the 5-yard line, take the touchback off the table and force returners to run every time, assuming that they'll be tackled before the 25.

And the Patriots did this strategy to great success with the majority of their kick-offs never getting past the 25-yard line and partly leading to another Super Bowl winning season. This is just one of the many examples of Belichick's rulebook knowledge that has led to many championships for the Patriots franchise. He knows the rules and how to use them to win games.

You know, financial planning is a lot like that. If you want to create a solid investment portfolio, plan for retirement or a big purchase, and win the tax game, you need to keep mistakes to a minimum and understand the different rules and investment options to have success.

In Canada, the two best options for saving money long-term is the RRSP and TFSA. Let's put them in the boxing ring and see which heavyweight wins this decision.

Fight Night: RRSP vs. TFSA

The Registered Retirement Savings Plan (RRSP) is an account registered with the Government of Canada that is designed to encourage and help Canadians save for retirement. The RRSP was long the staple for Canadians retirement savings.

Then in 2009, along came the Tax-Free Savings Account (TFSA), which suddenly provided a second, option to shelter retirement savings.

This created a GOAT-like debate (GOAT standing for Greatest of All Time) similar to what people have with Jordan vs. LeBron or Gretzky vs. Lemieux or Smooth vs. Chunky peanut butter. You get the picture.

Should I use a TFSA or a RRSP is one of the most common questions people ask. Both are great savings vehicles and have their advantages but depending on your situation, one might be better than the other.

The RRSP offers greater tax benefits under the right circumstances but there are some features such as paying income tax when you withdraw that make it less flexible.

The TFSA may not provide as many tax benefits as the RRSP but since withdrawing money out of it has no tax consequences, it is much more flexible.

RRSP Basics

In simple terms, an RRSP is an account designed to help Canadians save for retirement. And with a shrinking number of Canadian employers providing employee-sponsored pension plans, RRSPs are more important than ever. The money you put in an RRSP can be used to buy a range of investment options - mutual funds, ETFs, stocks, bonds and such. While these investments are being held in your RRSP, you won't have to pay tax on any interest, dividends, or capital gains you earn.

Because RRSPs are government registered accounts, they are subject to certain rules. One of the rules is you are limited in the amount of money you can contribute to the account in a given year. The amount changes, but for example in 2018, the maximum money you can contribute is 18% of your income or $26,230 - whichever is smaller. If you didn't max out in previous years, you can check your Notice of Assessment to find out how much you can contribute.

Another feature that makes RRSPs such great savings tools is the ability to reduce your income tax with your contributions. You can subtract the amount you contribute from your income and pay less in income taxes. For example, if you made $70,000 and you contributed $10,000 to your RRSP, you will pay tax on only $60,000 of income.

You're probably now thinking, "Hooray! This sounds amazing but there has to be some catch, right?"

You will eventually have to pay taxes when you withdraw your money but the strategy is that when you do so, you'll be retired and your tax rate will be lower. This point is **very important**: The way to use RRSPs properly is to make sure your tax bracket is high when contributing but that your tax bracket is low when you withdraw from it.

TFSA Basics

The TFSA is a simpler tool that allows your investments to grow and withdraw tax-free but doesn't provide the tax-deduction benefits of the RRSP. It's great for objectives that are earlier than retirement, but you can also use the account for retirement in certain cases.

Just like the RRSP, the TFSA can be invested in a variety of investment vehicles from ETFs to Mutual Funds to

GICs. The main benefit is obviously right in the name - you don't pay taxes on the money you make. And unlike your Registered Retirement Savings Plan, you can take money out of your TFSA any time you want with no tax repercussions. If you do take out money, the amount is added to how much you can contribute the following year.

The TFSA does come with some limits being a government registered account. There is a limit to how much you can contribute, right now at a maximum of $6,000 per year (as of 2020). You are eligible to start as soon as you're 18 years old. But yeah, that's pretty much the only downside so it's not a question of "Should I open a TFSA?" it is "Wow, I should definitely open a TFSA and start investing!!!"

TFSAs are great for many different scenarios such as:

1. Investing towards an objective that is sooner than retirement (house, wedding, vacation, etc).
2. Investing for retirement and making less than $50,000/yr
3. Investing for retirement and making more than $50,000 but anticipate salary rising significantly. Using the TFSA now can defer RRSP room for later when salary is higher and take advantage of a greater tax deduction.
4. During retirement, the money withdrawn from a TFSA isn't considered income, so retirees can take out money without it affecting retirement benefits like OAS which decreases with higher income.

And the Winner Is??

It's a draw!!! Both the RRSP and TFSA are great for different purposes and life stages. You can use the RRSP to save for the long-term retirement that you deserve and the TFSA can allow for flexibility on the journey to retirement. When you get tax refunds from RRSP contributions, I know it is tempting to go buy the latest Bauer hockey stick but take care of your future self and put the refund in your TFSA for more money working towards you and your goals.

In the end, whatever account you are using - save, save, save!

17. HANGING UP THE JERSEY (RETIREMENT)

'Say goodbye to tension and hello to pension' - Unknown

Finding the balance of enjoying Now and Then

The phrase above is a perfect representation of the conflict that encompasses almost every financial decision in your life. The struggle is real. Finding that balance between enjoying life now and ensuring there is resources to enjoy life later is one of the toughest problems to solve.

There are some people that take this struggle to the extreme. There are some people who spend everything, save nothing, live paycheck to pay check and never plan for their future selves. Then there are others who are so frugal, never spend money and never enjoy or treat themselves. In the end, there has to be a balance.

This debate also plays out in sports, specifically around superstar players in their prime being compared to all-time greats.

Take LeBron James for example. I don't think I have ever seen another player more divided about their greatness than LBJ. He is arguably one of the greatest players to step on the basketball court and his whole career has been compared to other NBA legends like Michael Jordan and Magic Johnson. He has done some incredible things on and off the basketball court yet people will still not be impressed when comparing to other players or they are too caught up in the hoopla that they shove history aside.

Truth is, when players like this come along, there needs to be the same balance of enjoying the present greatness now while still respecting the past and future. If we spend too much time predicting how LeBron will finish his career or compare him to the past, we are missing out on great basketball as we speak. Players come and go in a short amount of time so enjoying the present while still looking towards the future and past is important for pure enjoyment of the players that play in sports.

As I write this book, I am now 26. I've been a saver all my life and I think that mindset was installed by my family and being mindful of my resources. Balance for me has been reminding myself that it's okay to spend money now and then to enjoy myself. Because life with a full bank account but no experiences or enjoyment is pointless.

I'm still a young person who should enjoy my life. In fact, everyone should. I understand how hard it is for money to come in but it flies out so easily. I appreciate and value money and saving for future goals but I make sure I take time to enjoy life in the here and now. Seeing both the now and the future and combining both into a balanced financial picture makes other parts of life fall into place so much better.

At the end of the day, you're only the age you are right now once. It's important to give 100 percent towards your career or schooling but to also take downtime to enjoy life, family and friends, travel and invest in other people.

No you can't have every single thing you want and even if you did, that won't ever make you truly satisfied. There really is no perfect way to figure out how much to save versus how much to spend but here are some thoughts on the topic.

Pay down debt, or save for retirement?

The "how much do I need to retire?" question was thrown out earlier in the book where the answer I gave depended on a lot more questions and variables.

You obviously have to save, save, save to create a pool of capital throughout your working years that can create a reasonable lifestyle during your retirement years.

Many people are faced with the question of whether to put savings into a retirement plan or use them to pay down debt.

Well there is some good news: building your retirement plan or paying down debt are both good options!

So once again, it can come down to different priorities and scenarios that can help you throughout your decision making process.

First, you have to look at your situation and ask some questions to yourself. How much debt do you have? What are interest rates? How much savings do you have? Are you only making minimum payments? Are you stressed about your finances?

Next would be to create a plan based on your priorities. The best-case scenario would be to address both debt and savings at the same time. If your workplace provides a matching RRSP account then that is a no-brainer to enrol in. When tackling both debt and retirement at the same time you cover off your future and the now. You can always allocate a bit more funds to whatever preferences you have as well.

In the end, putting money towards both is the best idea for anyone because no one wants debt forever and no one wants to work forever. Savings for the future like retirement is important.

The retirement game is very exciting but can also leave a lot of people stressed about so many unknowns.

All the uncertainty of things like taxes, healthcare costs, inflation and life expectancy come into play making it a real guessing game.

The government's giant debt situation and baby boomers getting older will most likely lead to higher tax rates down the road (as if they weren't high enough already!). And benefits such as CPP and OAS will continue to get stingier as the older population and debt puts pressure on these luxuries.

And this comes all with the fact that people want to retire earlier and earlier while living longer and longer.

The Extreme Early Retirement Movement

It's hard to see a week go by without seeing a news report or blog on someone being profiled on how they retired at an extremely young age.

These people generally have an abnormally high savings rate (somewhere in the 50%-80% range) to go along with an abnormally low spending rate and very minimalist lifestyle. These people are retiring in their 30's after a period of ultra-extreme saving.

First of all, total respect to these people that are doing this. Saving money is an extremely tough thing to do and there are so many people out there today who are not saving any money at all. For these people to be able to save enough money to be financially independent at such young ages requires a combination of discipline, hard work and planning that is very rare these days.

I think the main thing for these people is they could never find the "work-life balance" realm they were looking for. Many of these people didn't like their jobs, either working too many hours, high stress or didn't like their employer. Most were looking to save enough so they could get out to do work they wanted to be doing. If you find or are already in a career you love, there's no reason to look for an early exit in your 30's.

In addition, I don't think extreme saving and not spending necessarily brings balance either. Balancing the need for enjoyment and delayed gratification is a tricky act. In addition to saving a lot of money to retire early there are also more factors to consider such as:

- Your money has to last you a long time
- Most of your money will be in taxable accounts
- Expenses tend to rise as you age
- Investment management becomes more important

These factors have solutions for them that can work but can become very difficult with 50-60 years to work with.

I'm not completely looking down on the extremely early retirement because I have full respect for the discipline it takes to get there. But I think financial independence has a different meaning than having enough savings to retire young.

I think financial independence means having enough to not stress about money all the time. Having enough so an out-of-the-blue expense won't be a big issue. And even having enough to treat yourself every once in a while without feeling guilty.

Setting specific financial and personal goals is very important and unique for everyone. When you understand who you are before making big financial commitments, you will have a rich life no matter what you decide to do.

Save & Enjoy

Whenever I have received extra income or a bonus, my strategy has been to save a decent chunk to get it working for my future but also carving out a piece to spend some of it now in an enjoyable way.

The best teams are always reloading and preparing themselves for the future to continue their success. They will do this by getting draft picks to prepare their minor league system and develop into players that will be ready when the opportunity comes. Some might be trading for specific players that could help the team now or in the future. It is a constant balance to find but once a system or strategy is in place, success comes with it.

One of the best strategies to save and enjoy at the same time is to automate savings. By doing this you will be saving money while also taking away the temptation to spend it in the first place. This is huge from a psychological standpoint to make saving less painful. It allows you to spend money without feeling guilty about it because you're simply using what's left over. This can also create opportunity to spend more on things that make you happy and cut back on other areas that aren't a priority.

We're all dealing with finite resources so we should be spending our discretionary income on the things and experiences that bring us the most joy. When spending money, look at what will bring the biggest bang for your hard earned buck.

I know many people like me will focus on savvy savers and those that invest well but there are wise spenders out there too which I think is important to note when looking at the other side of the save/spend equation.

And you don't have to be cheap, just smartly make purchases as investments and seek the highest available return. Not measuring return in dollars or percentages, but in joy.

Here's an example. Perhaps you go get a $5 Starbucks twice a week throughout the course of a 4 week month. That's $40 after one month and gives you a little bit of joy while you drink it. But what about if you spend that $40 on let's say a Raptors game or a round of golf with some friends and you feel much more joy and exuberance? Would that not be the greater return on investment?

Just as being a better saver is important, choosing how to spend your money better is also important. You will have to spend money in life there is no doubt. By learning how to prioritize, think before spending and not keep up with the Joneses, you will be able to wisely spend your money on things or experiences that bring a higher return of happiness and joy.

18. PUTTING IT ALL TOGETHER

"The future ain't what it used to be."
- Yogi Berra

We all try to over think many things in life. We look at things that are easy and try to make it more complex because if it were that easy then everyone would be doing it. While something can be said for coaches that design creative new plays or schemes, it also usually comes with more risk of not turning out. When looking at your finances, risk is a scary word, not that you should completely run from it but make sure the risks taken are warranted. Everything needs to be aligned with your game plan towards your goals.

The best coaches in sports have game plans with players, plays and systems all set out for specific scenarios that will help achieve their final goals. Having a plan in place for your finances, estate and other assets doesn't mean it's set in stone, but gives direction and purpose to become successful. Those that aimlessly invest or turn a blind eye towards these topics provide a sure way to fail. As Benjamin Franklin said "failing to plan is planning to fail."

In essence, this chapter tries to ensure that you don't need to overcomplicate things when putting your financial picture together. Basic things such as putting plenty into retirement, getting out from any high-interest debt and so forth or scenarios that don't need to be confusing, they just need to get done.

Why Simple Beats Complex

Kentucky Wildcats men's basketball coach John Calipari has a goal set out every year for his team to win the national championship and have his player's progress successfully to the NBA. To make the greatest impact, each member of the team must come together; align their goals and work as a team in order for everyone to be successful.

It's not all about having flashy dunks, fancy passes or the highest vertical. Instead, trust in the process, caring about the team and keeping it simple will bring success. You want to limit the mistakes and errors and for the most part, simplicity will win in the long run.

When it comes to financial planning or investing, try not to over think it. If you try to make your process too complex, you will never stick to it. Or it may work once but never again.

When putting together an investment portfolio, trying hard to make it complex does not guarantee better results. In fact, by trying to make it more complex, you open yourself up to more possibilities that bring about consequences. Outsmarting the competition is easier said than done because that doesn't actually make you a better investor. Just ask the Harvard Endowment portfolio managers.

Harvard Blew $1 Billion on Brazilian Tomatoes

In 2012, Harvard managers invested a large amount of money in an agricultural development in Brazil (McDonald & Freitas, 2018). The workers in this land would produce tomato paste, sugar and ethanol. The thinking was that these profits could perform better than conventional stocks and bonds, add a new level of diversification outside the stock market and keep the world's richest university ahead of its peers.

6 years later and Harvard looks like big losers after writing down over $1 billion on its natural resources portfolio (McDonald & Freitas, 2018). Harvard believed that its money managers were smarter than everyone else and that they could handle this risk that others avoided.

Source: Bloomberg (McDonald & Freitas, 2018)

Harvard's over the 10-year period from 2007-2017 even lagged the simplest approach - investing in a market tracking index fund holding 60 percent stocks and 40 percent bonds which earned an annual 6.4%.

The basic lesson is even the best of the best make mistakes. Keeping it simple - low costs and diversify - can provide great returns for your goals over time.

Make it a Golfers Game

THE GAME PLAN

For anyone that's played golf, golf can be a long game. Hence, there can be some great lessons to learn from this game that can also hold true in investing: from the risks and rewards of taking an aggressive shot to over-thinking a decision because of too much analysis.

Most pro golfers like Brooke Henderson will stick to a strategy throughout a tournament that comprises shots they have practiced combined with the occasional aggressive potentially high reward play. This can become the same with investors.

The world's top golfers have a plan for every round they play - which clubs to hit at certain distances, when to be aggressive, when to play it safe and stick to the fundamentals. Great golfers have great fundamentals (exception Bubba Watson who is a pure natural). Things such as grip, swing plane or impact position are practices over and over to become natural and automatic.

Having strong investing fundamentals are essential for creating a strong portfolio. Understanding your investing goals, required rate of return and tolerance for risk brings about decisions on how to structure your financial plan.

Having a trusted person for advice can also help if you are not fully comfortable with managing it on your own. Mentioned earlier in the book that even the pros have coaches and caddy's that provide expert advice for continuous improvement. Make sure it is someone you can trust, do a thorough research and that you agree with their philosophy to make a positive experience.

19. LAST MINUTE OF THE GAME

"There's winning and there's losing and in life you have to know that they both will happen. But what's never been acceptable to me is quitting."
- Magic Johnson

THE GAME PLAN

Last minute of play in the 3rd period. Bottom of the ninth inning. 2-minute warning in football. Last minute in March madness. Match point in tennis. 18th hole in golf. Final 10 metres in the swimming pool.

Every sports game comes to an end. This is where the game is decided on who wins and who loses (even tie's for soccer fans). The game is either a blowout and the decision is known or it can be a close, nail-biting finish. When the game gets closer to the end, that's sometimes the most exciting moments in sports.

While I hope you really don't want this book to come to an end, I hope to try and end on some last minute tips and make sure the next moment in your financial game is set up for success.

Make the Easy Lay-Up (Or if You're Shaq's Height, the Easy Slam Dunk)

As we've seen throughout this book, there are so many decisions and choices to make when it comes to our finances. It can be overwhelming to think of how each route we take with our finances can affect our well being and ability to achieve our goals. And as the world constantly tries to make itself more complex, keeping things simple at the end of the day leads to the best results.

You see in sports people try to take difficult shots or plays when the simple play is the most effective. Throwing the ball deep on every football play has a lower success rate than handing off the ball to your running back and getting good yards to set you up for more plays.

Making the easy layup instead of trying a fancy, turnaround, no-look jump shot will also have a higher percentage of success and get you the same amount of points on the basket.

With your finances you can't afford to take uncalculated risks such as stock-picking, not saving, or abusing lines of credit because that can restrict yourself from achieving the lifestyle and goals you want.

When investing, it's important to realize that no one knows what returns stocks and bonds will deliver in the years ahead. And when people debate passive vs. active investing, I think it more comes down to simple vs. complex and high-probability portfolios vs. low-probability portfolios.

Investing is hard enough as it is before bringing in complex, inefficient, low-probability investment styles.

That's why I believe that despite all the inevitable uncertainty surrounding the world of investing, there remain lots of common sense realities that we do know.
- The simple 'lay-up', 'run the ball' with high-probability investing style wins.
- We know that we must start investing at the earliest possible moment and continue to invest regularly from then on. Compound interest is a miracle. Time is your friend. Give yourself all the time that you possibly can.
- We know investing brings about risk. But we also know that not investing is a sure-fire way to fail to

accumulate the wealth necessary to ensure a sound financial future.
- We know that costs and taxes matter and must minimize them.
- We know that beating the market or successfully timing the market has proven to be ineffective and unsuccessful over long-term and success has only been done by few not many.

You can read all the financial books and blogs you want, take all the advice from as many different experts but the main ideas will always stay the same. What I hope this book brought you is a new way to think about these financial terms by bringing sports into the picture. Using different analogies and situations in sport, allows for a clearer understanding of how to navigate these simple components to a balanced financial life.

We can listen to all the simple, but not easy, financial advice such as: diversify, keep costs low, spend less, save more, stop watching the stock markets, work less on investing, not more but it all comes down to not being fancy.

Arguably the greatest personal finance book, *The Wealthy Barber* by David Chilton, sums up strong financial plans in a story of a farmer's financial plan. All the pieces such as living within their means, using RRSPs and compounding led them to achieving all the goals and success they wanted. They got there not by doing anything fancy, just discipline and good financial awareness.

Just as in sports, success in personal finance comes down to a few main things:

THE GAME PLAN

Play the game right.

Keep it simple.

Know the rules.

Control what you can control.

Be patient

Stay disciplined.

Play until the final whistle or until the horn sounds.

The End.

The views and opinions expressed in this book belong solely to Bryton Keyes. All investment strategies, and future gains and losses are taken at your own risk and Bryton is not held accountable.

References:

Anderson, A., Baker, F., & Robinson, D. (2016). Precautionary Savings, Retirement Planning and Misperceptions of Financial Literacy. *Swedish House of Finance Research Paper,15*(1). doi:10.3386/w21356

Arthur, R. (2016, February 29). The Shrinking Shelf Life of NFL Players. Retrieved October 14, 2018, from https://www.wsj.com/articles/the-shrinking-shelf-life-of-nfl-players-1456694959

Birch, M. (2018, February 05). Tom Brady reacts to Eagles' key strip-sack fumble in Super Bowl LII. Retrieved April 14, 2020, from https://thesportsdaily.com/2018/02/05/tom-brady-reacts-to-eagles-key-strip-sack-fumble-late-in-super-bowl-lii/

Cardone, G. (2018, August 30). Warren Buffett has made 99.7% of his money after the age of 52. Retrieved October 14, 2018, from https://medium.com/the-10x-entrepreneur/warren-buffett-has-made-99-7-of-his-money-after-the-age-of-52-71e2ce04c347

Chase, C. (2016, November 15). HOW BILL BELICHICK IS EXPLOITING THE RULE BOOK AND WHY THE NFL HAS TO STOP IT IMMEDIATELY. Retrieved from https://amp.foxsports.com/stories/nfl/how-bill-belichick-is-exploiting-the-rule-book-and-why-the-nfl-has-to-stop-it-immediately

Constable, S., & Espinoza, J. (2014, September 14). Mutual Funds' Five-Star Curse: Most Top-Rated Funds Lose Their Crown. Here are Seven Lessons for Investors. *The Wall Street Journal.*

Dimson, E., Marsh, P., & Staunton, M. (2018). *Credit Suisse Global Investment Returns Yearbook 2018*(pp. 1-41, Rep.). Zurich, Switzerland: Credit Suisse Research Institute.

Duffy, T. (2017, September 12). Gregg Popovich Gives Classic Interview After 1st Quarter vs. Heat. Retrieved November 12, 2018, from https://bleacherreport.com/articles/2615447-gregg-popovich-gives-classic-interview-after-1st-quarter-vs-heat

Elkins, K. (2017, May 09). 11 of Warren Buffett's funniest and most frugal quirks. Retrieved November 15, 2018, from https://www.cnbc.com/2017/05/09/11-of-warren-buffetts-funniest-and-most-frugal-quirks.html

Elkins, K. (2017, September 29). NFL star Kirk Cousins earns $24 million a year and spends summers in his parents' basement. Retrieved August/September, 2018, from https://www.cnbc.com/2017/09/29/nfl-star-kirk-cousins-spends-summers-in-his-parents-basement.html

ESPN. (2014). The Mag's Ultimate Standings 2014. Retrieved December 12, 2018, from http://www.espn.com/sportsnation/teamrankings/_/year/2004

Fabrikant, G. (2008). Keep It Simple, Says Yale's Top Investor. Retrieved August 14, 2018, from http://www.nytimes.com/2008/02/17/business/17swensen.html

FanSided Staff. (2018, February 04). Tom Brady: Super Bowl 52 postgame quotes. Retrieved July 14, 2018, from https://fansided.com/2018/02/04/super-bowl-52-tom-brady-interview/

Giordano, A. (2018, January 4). Tee yourself up for investing success. Retrieved May 14, 2018, from https://www.vanguardcanada.ca/individual/articles/education-commentary/investing/tee-yourself-up-for-investing-success.htm

Gould, S. J. (2004). Why No One Hits .400 Any More. In *Triumph and tragedy in Mudville: A lifelong passion for baseball*. London: Cape.

Gray, W. (2017, August 19). Mission Impossible: Beating the Market Forever. Retrieved July 14, 2018, from https://alphaarchitect.com/2014/11/18/mission-impossible-beating-the-market-forever/

Mazda. (2017, April 20). Alfred Morris' 1991 Mazda 626. Retrieved May 12, 2020, from https://insidemazda.mazdausa.com/drivers-life/my-mazda-my-story/alfred-morris-mazda-626/

Mcclure, S. M., Ericson, K. M., Laibson, D. I., Loewenstein, G., & Cohen, J. D. (2007). Time Discounting for Primary Rewards. *Journal of Neuroscience,27*(21), 5796-5804. doi:10.1523/jneurosci.4246-06.2007

McDonald, M., & Freitas, T. (2018, March 01). Harvard Blew $1 Billion in Bet on Tomatoes, Sugar, and Eucalyptus. Retrieved October 26, 2018, from https://www.bloomberg.com/news/articles/2018-03-01/harvard-blew-1-billion-in-bet-on-tomatoes-sugar-and-eucalyptus

Reyes, L. (2018, February 05). Tom Brady sets Super Bowl record for passing yards in a game in Patriots' loss to Eagles. Retrieved April 14, 2018, from https://www.usatoday.com/story/sports/nfl/2018/02/04/tom-brady-super-bowl-passing-record-patriots-eagles/305836002/

Rollins, K. (2019, January 02). With Harvard as the Backdrop, NBA Players Learn Business from the Best and Brightest. Retrieved August 14, 2019, from https://ca.sports.yahoo.com/news/harvard-backdrop-nba-players-learn-173021045.html?guccounter=1

Saslow, E. (2015, March 5). From The Mag: Top MLB prospect lives by his own rules. Retrieved August 12, 2018, from http://www.espn.com/espn/feature/story/_/id/12420393/top-blue-jays-prospect-daniel- norris-lives-own-code

Stevenson, A., & Goldstein, M. (2017, May 01). John Paulson's Fall From Hedge Fund Stardom. Retrieved October 26, 2018, from https://www.nytimes.com/2017/05/01/business/dealbook/john-paulsons-fall-from-hedge-fund-stardom.html?referer=https%3A%2F%2Ft.co%2FJ2auLdbeCT

Torre, P. (2009, March 23). How (and Why) Athletes Go Broke - Sports Illustrated Vault. Retrieved September 12, 2018, from https://www.si.com/vault/2009/03/23/105789480/how-and-why-athletes-go-broke

Zweig, J. (2015, November 16). Saving Investors from Themselves. Retrieved June 12, 2018, from http://jasonzweig.com/saving-investors-from-themselves-2/

Zweig, J. (2016, November 12). Can't Save? Blame Your Brain. Retrieved September 12, 2018, from http://jasonzweig.com/cant-save-blame-your-brain/

ABOUT THE AUTHOR

Bryton Keyes is an MBA graduate from Wilfrid Laurier University working towards his CPA in Assurance at Ernst & Young. Always a big sports fan, he has worked for Maple Leafs Sports & Entertainment and the BC Lions Football Club. He plays many sports including hockey, golf, volleyball, tennis and spikeball. While working in Wealth Management he found the natural connections between sports and finance fascinating and a useful tool when communicating to clients. He lives with his wife and new baby boy in Kitchener, Ontario.

Made in the USA
Columbia, SC
29 November 2020